Careers in Entertainment & Sports

By J. Michael Ribas

2006 Edition

WetFeet Insider Guide

WetFeet ®

Helping you make smarter career decisions.

WetFeet, Inc.

The Folger Building
101 Howard Street
Suite 300
San Francisco, CA 94105

Phone: (415) 284-7900 or 1-800-926-4JOB
Fax: (415) 284-7910
Website: www.WetFeet.com

Careers in Entertainment & Sports

By J. Michael Ribas
2006 Edition
ISBN: 1-58207-532-8

Table of Contents

Entertainment and Sports at a Glance

Opportunity Overview

- Undergraduates and those without experience compete for internships (often unpaid), which frequently segue into permanent positions on the business side of the industry.

- The industry offers many assistantships—jobs that typically involve long hours, low pay, and lots of grunt work, but also give smart, dedicated go-getters the opportunity to learn the business.

- An advanced degree does not necessarily qualify a candidate for high-profile work. For law school grads and MBAs, entertainment companies' marketing, finance, and legal departments offer assistantships with substantial responsibilities. A JD is useful when working as a sports agent, and MBAs are prized by the major leagues.

- Midcareer professionals should work their industry contacts or consult with industry-specific recruiters to learn about open positions in marketing, finance, legal, publicity, production, and human resources. Be aware, though, that it's not easy for people to enter entertainment from other fields. It's somewhat easier to enter sports if you have experience in a function that will translate.

Major Pluses

- You work on projects that are seen and heard by millions of people.

- The culture of most entertainment and sports companies is youthful, energetic, and, in the case of entertainment, highly creative.

- Although entry-level employees can expect to toil several years in administrative positions, entertainment and sports careers allow for rapid advancement in rank and compensation for the ambitious (and lucky).

Major Minuses

- Aside from the growing opportunities at record labels in Nashville, most jobs at major film studios, television networks, and music labels are in New York or Los Angeles. You have to relocate if you're not a resident, and at the lower levels, compensation for most positions is lower than for similar positions in many other industries. Though sports opportunities are more spread out geographically than those in the film, music, and television arenas, the salaries are comparably low.

- Experience in the entertainment and sports industry doesn't translate well to other fields. If you decide you want to switch fields, you may have to start at the bottom . . . again.

- In film, music, and television, there are a lot of ego-driven people who like to think of themselves as geniuses—and the strong personalities may test your patience. In sports, the people are great but the hours are grueling.

The Industry

Overview

Your peers boast of plum positions in management consulting and investment banking, but you're not impressed. Since you were a kid, you've dreamed of working in television, film, music, or sports. Unfortunately, you stopped playing oboe in junior high school, you find standing in front of a camera and pretending you're someone else as pleasurable as a tooth-cleaning, and you do most of your quarterbacking on Monday morning in the office, not Sunday night on the playing field. You don't have to let that stop you, though—you can get in on the excitement by working on the business side of entertainment and sports.

Every year, hundreds upon thousands of job seekers flood Los Angeles and New York seeking jobs in entertainment. They soon find that despite the myth of effortless work and exorbitant salaries, the norm for entry-level employees is long days, low wages, and an ample dose of drudgery. Though sports-business hopefuls don't necessarily have to trek to these meccas to enter their field of dreams, the challenges they face are similar. And they may need to change locales at least once or twice to advance their careers. In either industry, there are exciting and high-paying business jobs to be had, but it takes hard work, an undying passion for what you do (or want to end up doing), and good luck to get them.

Before going any further, let's define what we mean by the entertainment industry. With the rise of the Internet and other new communications technologies, the field is increasingly difficult to define, but in this Insider Guide we're talking about film, television, and music, as well as sports—each a form of entertainment raking in millions of dollars. The first three of these businesses are dominated by enormous, vertically integrated companies such as Sony, Time Warner, and Walt Disney, which have interests in multiple segments of the industry. But there are also thousands of jobs in the entertainment industry at smaller, less corporate companies—film and television production or distribution companies, for instance, and small independent record companies, talent agencies, and management companies. Similarly, pro sports is dominated by the four biggest spectator sports—baseball, football, basketball, and hockey—but there are many other sports out there with varying degrees of business sophistication, and even at the Big Four there are numerous, albeit unglamorous and low-paying, jobs in minor-league outfits.

> ❝❞ **Someone who's an intern today can be your boss next week. That's the way it works in this business.**

Because of the variety of film, television, and music employers, it's impossible to speak in absolutes about what it's like to work in the entertainment industry. In general, though, you'll find it's dominated by a young workforce—especially as television and film focus more and more on young audiences. Many entertainment companies offer creative, unstructured work environments that allow rapid advancement for ambitious types; this is an industry that rewards bottom-line success much more than it does loyalty or tenure. As an insider says, "Someone who's an intern today can be your boss next week. That's the way it works in this business." And people who are successful in the industry find that entertainment is more a lifestyle than a profession; to remain plugged in, you have to spend much of your leisure time networking with fellow industry professionals or attending industry parties. "You have to give up your life to deal with the reality of the business," an insider says.

In sports, career advancement is glacial by comparison. There are a lot of people who love what they're doing and have found a way to live with the low salaries. Also, it's extremely hard to rise to the very top because sports organizations are all privately owned, and the owners tend to put their people—relatives, even—into the top slots.

You'll find plenty of competition for jobs in entertainment and sports. While the number of entertainment companies and related operations has grown exponentially since the early '90s, the industry is no longer in an expansion phase. Film studios are cutting back on project budgets and the number of movies they produce, and record companies are reducing staff and the number of artists on their rosters—which means fewer opportunities for those looking to break in. Sports companies are still expanding, but even so, for each lower-level major-league position that opens up, there are still at least 100 resumes that come in per job opening.

Take heart, though. These companies can't afford to neglect talented people. If you prove that you have the qualities and skills to thrive in this industry, you will find a place in television, movies, music, or sports. For undergraduates, the best avenue in is an internship. The compensation—if any—will be low and the work clerical. Most major companies require that interns be enrolled students who can receive college credit for their stint, but some offer internships to recent college graduates. Interns do get some perks—free merchandise, an exciting work environment, and sometimes a chance to meet stars, and definitely a chance to meet athletes. More important, internships can lead to permanent employment.

If you don't have the option of working as an intern, don't despair. Entry-level and midcareer candidates without previous industry experience can land jobs if they're thorough and persistent. And consolidation and increasing sophistication are creating more opportunities for MBAs and law school graduates in the corporate marketing, finance, and legal departments.

Regardless of your level of expertise and education, you need to explore every avenue open to you, and keep following up on any job leads. One reason is that if you persevere through the difficulties of the job search, employers will recognize you as someone who will thrive in a challenging work environment.

The Bottom Line

The field of entertainment and sports encompasses some of the most competitive businesses around. Just looking for a job may exhaust you. Once you find one, you won't be very well compensated, at least to start. And then you'll probably spend the first years working like a dog at the bottom of a seemingly insurmountable string of obstacles. But if you're alert to the opportunities that crop up around you, a chance to demonstrate your talent will probably arise. If you prove yourself then, people will take notice, and you will most likely be rewarded.

People who work in entertainment and sports are usually not in it just for the job. They're in it because they have a passion for the product, whether it's an independent documentary film or the Super Bowl. If you're not passionate about your industry—or if a big starting salary, a structured environment, or a typical nine-to-five situation is important to you—you may want to consider another field.

Entertainment Industry Breakdown

As we move into the digital age, it's getting more difficult to cleanly break down the industry into traditional categories. One reason for this is the proliferation of new forms of entertainment—interactive media, the Internet, and the like. Another reason is that many film, television, and music companies have united to form entertainment conglomerates.

Because corporate ownership of entertainment companies can lead to an intensified focus on the bottom line, it has been a problem for some employees who are more concerned with quality than with profits. On the other hand, some insiders have seen their opportunities increase because of the growth of conglomerates in entertainment—now employees often have the ability to move to other entertainment divisions within the conglomerate they work for. Corporate ownership has also changed the playing field by creating positions for people with more traditional business backgrounds.

While the landscape of the industry is changing, for the purposes of this guide we break entertainment into three traditional categories—television, film, and music—and then follow these up with a look at sports entertainment as its own standalone category. (Because of space limitations, this Insider Guide does not discuss radio, local television, or videogames. Job seekers should be aware that there are plenty of opportunities in those fields, too.)

TELEVISION

Television is arguably the 20th century's most significant—and most popular—technological development. In 1945, there were fewer than 7,000 television sets in use in the United States. Today, almost every American household has a television, and two in three households have more than one. The number of channels and networks—and the number of jobs in television—has grown along with television's popularity. But competition for jobs in this segment of the entertainment industry remains particularly stiff. At the entry level, this translates into poor compensation. And although executives are paid generously, job security is always an issue in television. Most opportunities are in Los Angeles and New York, where the networks and major production companies are headquartered.

Broadcast

For most of television's existence, the three major broadcast networks—ABC, CBS, and NBC—have dominated the business. But the traditional broadcast networks have faced a number of challenges in the past 25 years. For one thing, they're up against competition for audiences from cable—and increasingly from the Internet as well. They're also dealing with competition from upstart broadcast networks like The WB and Fox; the latter has done so well in its short existence that many now consider it the fourth major network. And while the television networks are generating more revenue than ever, they're also paying more for programming. The star syndrome means that hot actors can demand astounding salaries—the six cast members of the hit television show *Friends* earned one million dollars each, per episode. And televised sporting events attract large audiences, but often not big enough to offset high production costs and expensive broadcast rights.

One answer seems to be to lower costs by producing more "reality" programming, like *Survivor* and *The Apprentice*. At the same time, dramas that don't rely on name stars, such as the shows in the *Law & Order* franchise, can provide good returns with lower overhead. That said, cost-cutting is the word behind the scenes, too, so none of the established networks are hiring as many or as often as before.

Job opportunities in broadcast television include positions in production, publicity and promotions, business and legal affairs, distribution, advertising sales, and programming development.

Cable

Cable channels and networks aim at more specific audiences than broadcast networks. For example, ESPN targets sports fans, and MTV targets pop music fans. While broadcast networks can charge higher advertising rates than cable channels and networks because they attract more viewers, cable channels and networks typically pay much less for programming—and are more profitable as a result. With digital television soon to be the standard, cable channels and networks appear to be the future of the medium. As an insider says, "The expansion of digital television means the extension of cable space and cable channels."

What this means for job seekers: Opportunities are on the rise in the cable sector. And because broadcast networks often hire people who have proven themselves at cable networks or channels, these can be good places to start if you eventually want to work at a broadcast network. Opportunities in the cable segment are similar to those in the broadcast television segment.

FILM

Before there was a television in every home, film was the medium that created a common national language. Taking weekend trips to the movie house to view double and triple features, and the newsreels that ran between each film, was a way of life for people in the '30s, '40s, and '50s. But television soon replaced the movies as the most popular entertainment medium. The movie industry for the most part remained stagnant until the release of *Jaws* in 1975. That film's gross revenue—more than $260 million domestically—and sensational special effects reinvigorated and redefined the film industry. Film studios rushed to make blockbusters, which cost millions of dollars to produce, but when successful could return more than $100 million in box office grosses.

The Studio System

The success of *Titanic*, the most expensive film ever made, with a budget of more than $200 million—a figure that doesn't even include marketing and advertising costs, which usually account for half a production's overall budget—emphasized the windfall potential of the blockbuster film. Although the major studios—which include MGM, Walt Disney, Paramount, 20th Century Fox, Universal, and Warner Brothers—each release an average of 20 films a year, only about a third of those films produce multi-million dollar returns. That means studios depend on the profits from a few successful films to finance their operations—everything from the production of box office duds to development work on films that never get made. Production cutbacks generally translate into fewer jobs for the freelancers who work on movie sets (camera operators, key grips, gaffers, and all those other people who show up deep in a movie's credits). As well, major film studios are not hiring as many office workers as they have in the past.

Opportunities in the studio system are at the studios themselves and at the production companies the studios develop films with and buy films from (e.g., Imagine Entertainment or Lucasfilm). Positions are in departments such as production, acquisitions, development, home video, international operations and sales, business and legal affairs, music, publicity and promotions, distribution, and marketing.

Independent Films

While the blockbuster has been a mainstay of the industry ever since the release of *Jaws*, character-driven independent films, or "indies," have enjoyed increasing success in the past decade, prompting the major studios to start investing in some smaller-budget films. Indie-inspired subsidiaries of major studios, such as Disney's Miramax, are producing the most commercially and artistically successful films, and they're where many industry insiders are looking for jobs. Expect lots of competition in this area.

A lot of people think that the independent film market got its start with Quentin Tarantino and the growth in popularity of the annual Sundance Film Festival in Park

City, Utah. But the independent film (generally considered to be a film made outside the studio system, with financing by the filmmaker or an independent production company) was actually born in the '60s and '70s, when filmmakers such as Martin Scorsese, Francis Ford Coppola, and Woody Allen were forced to work outside the studio system by their desire to make films that were cultural and political statements, not mere entertainment. Still, it's the bottom-line success of independent films in the past decade that's turned them into a bona fide force in the movie industry. As we've said, many studios now have subsidiaries dedicated to making indie-style, lower-budget, character-driven films. These divisions' releases are sometimes even called independent films, though they don't truly meet the definition. And even technically independent production companies may be closely tied to studios. Often, when an independent production company contracts with a studio to make a film, studio executives must approve major production decisions, particularly those involving finances.

The number and types of opportunities in independent filmmaking depend on the production company in question. Truly independent filmmakers arrange financing for their films themselves, sometimes through their own production companies, and have the tightest of budgets (and the fewest opportunities for jobseekers); the bigger indie production companies hire on more staff and offer better pay and more job security. A production assistant (PA) on an independent film usually earns less than a PA on a major studio movie; on the other hand, a PA on the set of an indie film is likely to get more responsibility because the crew is much smaller. If you're looking for a job doing something high-tech like computer animation, your best bet is to ignore independent studios and focus on the bigger-budget Hollywood players.

MUSIC

Technically, the recording industry got its start when Emile Berliner invented a prototype phonograph that recorded music. But the business of music really took off with the large-scale launch of a new technology—when radio stations started broadcasting in the '20s.

Today, the industry is dominated by large corporate music groups such as Warner Music Group, Universal, and Sony BMG. These companies produce most of the music in your local CD store's racks or your computer's hard drive, and tend to take advantage of—either through acquisition or pressing and distribution deals—any upstart labels that do particularly well in the marketplace. The most recent round of consolidation in the music industry brought independent labels in "outsider" genres such as rap and alternative rock into the major-label fold.

More than any other industry, the music industry relies on trends. In the early '90s, alternative and rap replaced metal and urban R&B music, and were in turn replaced by the teen pop of Britney Spears and various boy bands. Now that teen pop has petered out, industry professionals are heralding back-to-basics rock bands like the White Stripes and the low-key singer-songwriters like Norah Jones, a Grammy winner. However, neither the garage-band revival nor the jazzy-singer revival has sparked a wholesale revitalization of the industry.

The Major Music Groups

Sony BMG, Warner Music Group, EMI, and Universal Music Group own most of the world's largest record labels. (The labels owned by the companies are thus known as *major* labels.) Musicians typically denounce these corporations for regarding market share and profits as more important than artists and their music. Still, some industry insiders have faith in the major labels. According to an insider, "The good record companies balance integrity and commercial appeal. Projects are short-lived if they are just a product. You need to promote what someone is doing artistically."

Opportunities at record companies exist in departments including production, artists and repertoire (the people who recruit artists to the record label), legal, publicity and promotions, and distribution. The music conglomerates are more compartmentalized than the independent outfits. In other words, if you work in accounting at a major label, every aspect of your work will be accounting related; if you work in shipping at a smaller independent label, you might also recruit new bands or help promote existing bands. In addition, the majors have been downsizing, which means that opportunities can be hard to come by.

Independent Record Labels

Insiders see the entrepreneurial spirit of independent record labels as responsible for the most groundbreaking movements in the industry. As an insider says, "Selling for the mass market is giving people what they have already heard. You don't step on toes when you do this. Independent recording is really where cutting-edge methods and music are developing." In contrast to large music companies, the smaller labels are usually more focused on their artists and less concerned with the bottom line. They're often grass-roots organizations funded by friends and family, labors of love created to make music, not money. They're more willing to take risks with less mainstream sounds. These risks often fail, financially, at least, but when they succeed, they can launch whole new directions in music. Consider the successful new artists and sounds produced by small labels in the past half century, including Elvis Presley at Sun Records, Stevie Wonder at Motown, the Beastie Boys at Def Jam, and Nirvana at Sub Pop.

Positions at independent labels are similar to those at the big music companies, but the work is less focused than at the large entertainment conglomerates; your responsibilities will include many tasks not strictly part of your job description. By performing a range of tasks, you get a better sense of how the music business works and have more opportunities to take on responsibilities that lead to advancement. The downside is that moving from a small independent label to a large entertainment conglomerate can be difficult—you may not have the precise skills required to fill a more focused position, and you won't get the respect accorded those with major-label experience. Many small labels are located outside Los Angeles and New York, particularly country labels in Nashville.

DVD/HOME VIDEO

Home video, once a relative backwater in the film and music industries, and even less important in the television industry, is now a major revenue stream due to the advent of the DVD. Though the format had been in existence since 1997, it really took off with the DVD release of *The Matrix*, whose novel special features mesmerized early adopters and tech geeks. Home video became something to be owned, not simply rented. By 2003, home video made up 60 percent of major U.S. movie studios' revenue with consumer spending on DVD sales and rentals totaling $16 billion, a 40 percent increase over 2002. More than half of U.S. households now have DVD players, and ownership is increasing rapidly as prices come down.

Film studios are not the only ones to benefit from the explosive growth of this new format. In addition to the traditional revenue stream of syndication, TV studios can now release DVD boxed sets of old TV shows; there are now more than 1,300 TV series on DVD, representing 5 percent of all available DVD titles. Even the beleaguered music industry has benefited from the new format. DVDs of concerts and compilations of video-clips have compensated for shrinking CD sales, and in fact many CDs are now packaged with bonus DVDs to encourage purchase. Late 2004 saw the debut of the DualDisc format, which consists of a single disc with a CD surface on one side and DVD surface on the other.

As you might imagine, the success of the DVD is good news for jobseekers. Not only are the home-video departments of major studios booming, but independent companies that license TV, film, and music properties for DVD release have also sprung up in recent years.

Leaders in Film, Television, and Music

This table shows the major entertainment conglomerates and some of their respective, film, television, and music affiliates and/or subsidiaries.

Entertainment Industry Leaders

Entertainment Group (Parent Company)	Subsidiaries/Affiliates		
	Television	Film	Music
BMG (Bertelsmann AG)	none (Bertelsmann has international television holdings)	none (Bertelsmann has international film holdings)	Sony BMG (50%)
DreamWorks SKG	DreamWorks Television	DreamWorks Studios	none
EMI Group	none	none	Virgin, Capitol, Blue Note, Priority
NBC Universal (GE)	NBC, Bravo, USA, Sci Fi, MSNBC, Telemundo	Universal Pictures, Focus Features	none
News Corp.	B Sky B, Fox Broadcasting, Fox News Network, Fox Sports, DIRECTV	20th Century Fox Film, Fox Spotlight	Festival Mushroom Records
Sony Corp. of America (Sony Corp.)	Columbia Tri-Star Television	Columbia Tri-Star Motion Picture Group	Sony BMG (50%)
Time Warner	WB, HBO, TBS, CNN, TNT, Cinemax	Warner Brothers, Fine Line Cinema, New Line Cinema, Castle Rock	none
Viacom (National Amusement Inc.)	UPN, MTV, VH1, Nickelodeon, Nick at Nite, Showtime, The Movie Channel, The Sundance Channel, BET, Comedy Central, CBS	Paramount Pictures	none
Vivendi Universal	none	none	Universal Music Group

Entertainment Group (Parent Company)	Subsidiaries/Affiliates		
	Television	Film	Music
The Walt Disney Company	ABC, ESPN, Walt Disney TV	Walt Disney Pictures, Miramax, Touchstone Pictures	Hollywood Records, Mammoth Records
Warner Music Group	none	none	Atlantic Records Group, Warner Bros. Records

The following table ranks the leading entertainment companies by revenue.

Leading Entertainment Companies

Company	2004 Revenue ($M)	1-Year Change (%)	Employees
Sony Corp.	72,081	13.9	162,000
Time Warner	42,089	10.5	84,900
The Walt Disney Co.	30,752	13.6	129,000
Vivendi Universal	29,026	−9.4	55,451
Viacom	22,526	−15.3	38,350
News Corp.	20,450	1.8	38,000
NBC Universal	12,886	−10.7	n/a
EMI Group	3,872	13.1	7,996
Warner Music Group	2,548	−24.5	4,000
DreamWorks*	1,250	−31.1	1,100

*Revenue figures are estimates.
Note: Sony and EMI's fiscal year end is March; News Corp.'s is June; Disney and Warner Music Group's is September; and the rest have fiscal years ending in December.
Sources: Hoover's, WetFeet analysis.

Sports Industry Breakdown

The first distinction that must be made is between professional and amateur sports. Though this Insider Guide focuses on pro sports, high school and, in particular, college sports generate a lot of money and media attention at the local and regional levels. (Football is almost a religion through much of the South, for example.) Not only do high school and college sports provide prime training ground for future pro athletes, but they also perform a similar function for those wanting to work in the business side of sports. Ticket and advertising sales, facility administration, merchandising, radio and television rights, marketing, and PR: Many of the job functions found in pro sports have their counterparts here, and internships, part-time jobs, or full-time jobs in these areas look great on a resume.

In addition, you can gain entrée into a number of other amateur sports that, although they don't generate as much spectator attention, do have ardent followings: skiing, cycling, running, table tennis, and so on. If you have a passion for one of these sports, you can certainly build a career around that passion, though you likely won't get rich at it. (In fact, you might not be able to give up your day job.) However, if you have a talent for marketing, for example, you may be able to pair it with experience you've gained at, say, a rock-climbing association, and parlay that into a job at an outdoor sportswear manufacturer targeting that demographic.

THE BIG FOUR

At the professional level, the Big Four spectator sports (baseball, basketball, football, and hockey) are the giants in terms of fan interest, media attention, and revenue. Over the years, these sports have evolved so that each now has one dominant governing body (Major League Baseball, National Basketball Association, National Football League, and National Hockey League) reigning supreme. Originally, the main functions of the governing bodies were to create and enforce rules and policies regulating owners, players, and referees; to impartially organize games between teams; and to maintain statistics and issue awards to winning teams and outstanding players. While those functions remain, the incredible growth of sports as a revenue engine has propelled the governing bodies to become full-fledged businesses that encompass marketing and PR, logo licensing, television rights licensing, and revenue distribution among teams.

Teams are owned by, well, owners—usually several owners—who tend to be either wealthy individuals like Internet entrepreneur Mark Cuban (owner of the NBA's Dallas Mavericks) or entertainment companies such as Time Warner (owner of MLB's Atlanta Braves via Turner Broadcasting System). Owners hire and fire players in accordance with rules hammered out by the governing bodies and the players' associations, and owners are responsible for all marketing related to their teams and income streams such as ticket and concession sales, advertising, and merchandising.

The Big Four also own and operate minor league teams, which have their own governing bodies. Just as the collegiate teams do, minor league teams help many professionals break into the industry.

Opportunities in marketing, PR, merchandising, sales, operations, and other areas exist among teams and governing bodies. It is probably easier to break into the industry through a team than by any other route, since opportunities for internships and entry-level jobs are numerous in any city hosting professional teams. Be warned though, that competition remains fierce and pay is low.

SPORTS MANAGEMENT

The realization that companies would pay to be associated with the personality and achievements of pro golfer Arnold Palmer—and thereby increase their brand value—led his friend and financial manager Mark McCormack to almost single-handedly create the field of sports management, and the sports powerhouse IMG with it, in 1960.

A talent agent in the entertainment industry usually focuses on finding lucrative projects for his or her clients and then negotiating the best possible deal, but the sports agent (or sports manager) will often take the process one step further. Naturally, he or she will solicit or review offers from teams and negotiate contracts, but the real money is made off of the court (or field, or ice), in the form of endorsements. The name of the game is to get as much money as you can for the athletes you represent while they are still viable pitchmen—which, in most cases, means while they're still in the public eye as athletes. As Aaron Goodwin, NBA star Gary Payton's agent, puts it, "[A pro athlete and his agent are] a small corporation with a window of time to go out and get top dollar." The film *Jerry Maguire*, with its "Show me the money!" catchphrase, aptly illustrates the focus on maximizing revenue.

It wasn't until 1984 that sports management entered its golden age. That was the year Chicago Bulls rookie Michael Jordan entered into an endorsement deal with Nike. The resulting brand, Air Jordan, was a runaway success, and the company has been building ad campaigns, brands, and even retail outlets around the athlete ever since. Jordan also helped fuel Gatorade's preeminence in the sports-drink category. In 1991, when the Bulls superstar began pitching Gatorade, the company had $400 million in revenue. By 2002, that number had increased to $2 billion, due in large part to Jordan's endorsement activities. Nowadays, the number-one pitchman is Tiger Woods, whose yearly income from endorsements alone is estimated at more than $60 million. His biggest agreement is with Nike, a deal worth more than $100 million over a 5-year period set to end in 2005.

With numbers like these showing the upper end of the potential, it's no wonder that competition to represent athletes in endorsement deals is fierce—a 3 to 25 percent cut of the proceeds is the usual payoff. And not everyone manages to get a piece of the pie. Magnum Sports & Entertainment was forced to quit the sports businesses and is now reorganizing. TBA Entertainment also quit sports management, to focus on events management. Athletes can belly flop, too. NBA star Kobe Bryant, the third-largest earner after Woods and Jordan, may lose as much as $150 million dollars in future endorsement fees due to sexual assault charges filed against him in the summer of 2003.

At the top of the heap are integrated sports marketing and management companies like IMG. Big advertising companies have sought to diversify by either creating sports management companies, as Interpublic did with Octagon, or purchasing them outright, as Clear Channel did with SFX Sports Group. Traditional talent agencies such as the William Morris Agency also have sports practices. These agencies represent the biggest, most recognizable athletes in a wide range of sports.

INSIDER TIP

The name of the game is to get as much money as you can for the athletes you represent while they are still viable pitchmen—which, in most cases, means while they're still in the public eye as athletes.

A host of smaller sports management companies round out the field; these focus on a single sport or region. They tend to manage players of lesser stature, but with targeted, if limited, appeal. For example, a popular minor league player might have the kind of regional appeal that a smaller agency could successfully pitch to local businesses. Many of these companies are one-person shops, since practically anyone can be an agent. In fact, even a music mogul like rapper Master P was able to make a splash in 1999 by representing the NFL's Ricky Williams and several NBA players, though this arm of his business empire soon fell apart.

It should be no surprise that most people who enter this field are tax or contract lawyers, certified public accountants, or personal finance managers; basically, people who are comfortable with contracts, numbers, large sums of money, and the law. Some states require registration to help protect college athletes from getting taken advantage of; most professional players' associations offer agent certification to do the same for their members.

In fact, players' associations comprise another, albeit less-glamorous, area of sports management. These organizations are essentially unions that perform many functions on behalf of players: collective bargaining, disputing of fines and other punishments, seeking out of group sponsorship and endorsement deals, and financial and postcareer guidance. Players will sometimes go on to jobs at their players' association when they retire from their sport. People with union experience can also find jobs in this area.

SPORTS MARKETING

Sports marketing is a rather nebulous term for a number of activities in the sports world; pretty much every element of the sports industry is involved in marketing in one way or another. The powerhouses are the integrated sports management and marketing companies discussed previously. Naturally, an athlete's manager is closely involved with the marketing activities his client has signed on to as an endorser, to make sure that the athlete's brand image is not only maintained by the creative and positioning, but also enhanced and extended. Sometimes a sports marketer will get involved in as many facets of an opportunity as possible. For example, a company like IMG will not only create an event like Stars on Ice, but it will also get sponsorships from companies like Smuckers and tape the event for broadcast.

At the league level, sports marketers help companies market various consumer goods and services by allowing their logos, events, and players to be tied to marketing and advertising campaigns. In addition to direct revenue, there is also an extended benefit when the goods and services being marketed fit in well with a league's image. At the team level, sports marketers help the sales staff sell tickets and corporate sponsorships by building interest in the team through promotions, advertising, and game-day events that complement the game itself. They also help place the team name and logo on a variety of products—everything from caps to Coke cans—to maximize merchandising and sponsorship revenues and maintain a connection with fans. Public relations departments work with the media to get valuable coverage for games, players, promotional efforts, and human-interest stories, all of which enhance the team's appeal to fans and, by extension, to corporate sponsors.

On the other side of the fence sit companies that want to reach sports fans. Nike and Gatorade are far and away the sports-product companies that most actively market to sports fans, but the appeal of sports is so broad that beer companies such as Anheuser-Busch, automakers such as Ford, credit card companies such as VISA, and telecommunications companies such as AT&T are among the largest advertisers of televised sports events. The appeal is not limited to consumer goods companies, either. Technology-oriented companies like IBM and Nortel Networks advertise with and sponsor sports events in an attempt to put a human face on their businesses and reach busy corporate consumers during their downtime—and, it could be argued, when their guard is down. The biggest advertisers have dedicated sports marketing departments that find suitable advertising, promotional, and sponsorship efforts that will reach targeted consumers and, in the short term, turn them into customers while, over the long term, enhancing the company's or product's brand. A number of sports marketing companies, often with a particular focus, help smaller companies reach the niche they wish to capture.

Leading Sports Companies

Company	2004 Revenue ($M)	1-Year Change (%)	Employees
Nike	12,253	14.5	24,667
Adidas-Salomon	8,134	3.4	17,000
National Football League[1]	6,000	9.1	450
Interpublic Group[2,3]	5,863	−5.5	43,400
Major League Baseball[1]	4,100	7.9	n/a
Reebok International	3,785	8.6	9,102
NASCAR[1,4]	3,400	n/a	450
National Basketball Assn.[1]	3,000	n/a	n/a
Clear Channel Entertainment[2]	2,750	3.9	3,600
National Hockey League[1]	2,100	5.2	n/a
IMG[1,3]	1,200	−7.7	2,200
New Balance Athletic Shoe[1,3]	1,200	0.0	2,600
Bull Run Corp.[2]	55	−33.4	275

[1]Interpublic Group owns Octagon Sports, Clear Channel Entertainment owns SFX Sports, and Bull Run owns HOST Communications.

[2]Figures are estimates; these organizations do not publicly release financial information.

[3]Figures are from 2003. [4]Figures are from 2002.

Note: NFL and NHL's fiscal year end is March; Nike's is May; Bull Run's is June; MLB's is October; the rest are December.

Sources: Hoover's, WetFeet analysis.

Industry Trends

The major trend affecting the entertainment industry in recent years has been vertical integration. A few behemoth conglomerates, each of which combines various television, film, and music businesses under a single corporate umbrella, dominate the entire industry. (A side effect is that, with fewer companies, there are fewer top executives around, and enormous pressure is put on them to deliver results quickly. This has resulted in the dismissals of such media moguls as Vivendi Universal's Jean-Marie Messier, Time Warner's Robert W. Pittman, and Bertelsmann's Thomas Middelhoff.) Consolidation has made big entertainment seem more corporate and less creative than ever—although not nearly as much as in most other segments of corporate America. The upside is that, more than ever, employees have opportunities to move between different entertainment businesses—from a record label to a movie studio's music department, for instance. However, for every Sony Music–BMG merger, there is a Time Warner–Warner Music Group split; the shedding of noncore or underperforming divisions—even ones with blue-chip names—is now as much a valid business strategy as aggressive acquisitions are.

A number of other trends specific to certain segments of the entertainment industry are discussed here.

TELEVISION

Although broadcast networks still yield the highest ratings and generate more revenue than ever before, high programming costs are cutting into profits, and lower-overhead cable channels and networks are threatening to overturn broadcasting's dominance. The broadcast networks' parent companies are responding to these challenges by hiring people who can boost ad sales and cut costs. "Reality" programming continues to be another way for broadcasters to lower expenses; it's much cheaper to have a couple of cameras follow nonactors around all day, even in some exotic location, than to pay big salaries to talent and produce the usual sitcom or prime-time drama.

The heads of the major networks are also looking for new ways to generate revenue, such as demanding greater ownership of the programs they run, programs that are often made by independent production companies. With a bigger share of the shows, networks can make more money on selling them to affiliate stations. Executives are also increasing the longevity of programs by selling reruns to ancillary markets. In addition, the networks have bought their way into a number of cable operations, so the opportunities for employees to move from cable to broadcast—or vice versa—are even greater than before.

In terms of programming, broadcast networks are hiring people who have proven themselves at fledgling networks and channels. Although the networks desperately want to cut costs, one hit show can be the difference between the most and least successful networks. At the same time, NBC is bucking the custom of launching an entire slate of new programs—of which only a few will have any longevity—and filling in traditionally slow periods such as the summer with reruns. In 2004, the network announced that it would release just five new shows in the fall, and seven in the winter. This would not only limit reruns, but also give shows a less crowded playing field in which to find their audiences. If the strategy succeeds, jobs might be more stable, in line with a less-volatile programming schedule. In any case, the recent advertising slump has been improving—and as it does, you can expect job opportunities to improve, too. On a final note, sitcom writers who've felt left out in the cold because of the networks' reliance on reality programming will be encouraged by HBO's recent decision to move into sitcoms. If other cable channels follow suit, cable television might provide a haven for writers, not only by giving them jobs—which they need, since sitcoms have been all but disappeared from the Nielsen rankings recently—but by allowing them considerable leeway in subject matter and language.

FILM

The box-office success of independent films over the past few years has sparked significant changes in the film industry. Hollywood has bought into the appeal—and lower production costs—of character-driven films, and studios have established subsidiaries that solely produce such films. Consumers and critics alike have rewarded them for this endeavor. Moreover, many studio distribution departments are looking more seriously at foreign markets and other outside producers as sources of film "product"—partly because these ancillary sources are making movies that filmgoers are responding to, and partly because, when they buy a finished film, they have complete control over costs.

While these trends translate into less work for film crews, they heighten the demand for office personnel, who must find new writers, directors, and actors to put together these back-to-basics productions. "It takes talent to find talent," as the industry maxim goes. And studios' efforts to mimic the style of independent films and curtail production costs have meant less reliance on special effects and consequently a greater need for a steady stream of new writers, directors, and actors.

Cost-cutting aside, this is Hollywood we're talking about. Studios are still making special-effects extravaganzas—particularly for summer release—with generation after generation of new special-effects technologies. And industry giants such as Spielberg, Lucas, and Cameron continue to command $100 million budgets. However, studios now often employ joint-venture agreements with other studios to finance expensive films.

Studios are also more globally focused than ever, counting on foreign theater distribution and video sales to make up a significant portion of their films' revenues. Even a film that bombs at the domestic box office can end up making huge profits once its overseas revenue is included in the equation. (This is another reason the studios continue to produce blockbusters. After all, car chases and explosions don't require translation.) The downside is that much production has moved to Canada, Australia, and Eastern Europe, where labor costs are lower.

MUSIC

When Seagram followed its $10.4 billion purchase of PolyGram with the announcement that it would fire thousands of employees in a major restructuring, it initiated a trend among the major music groups (EMI, Sony BMG Music Entertainment, Universal Music Group, and Warner Music Group) toward making record label companies smaller and "smarter"—that is, focusing on a smaller number of "surefire" acts. Cuts will continue. In 2004, Sony Music and BMG merged to form Sony BMG Music Entertainment. (BMG had been in similar talks with Warner Music Group in 2003, but the two management teams couldn't get along.) This could leave Warner Music Group and EMI out in the cold, as the only two majors unable to find a dance partner. Or the resulting disparity between them and the Universal and Sony BMG behemoths may finally convince regulators that the only way they can survive is to join together.

In any case, the industry doldrums, which began in 2001, continue to put a damper on hiring. Though the television industry must contend with the commercial-skipping TiVo, and the movie industry has concerns about DVD piracy in Asia and Latin America, no industry is more paranoid about a technological advance eating into its profits than the music industry is about file sharing. With music sales down more than 20 percent since 2000, the major labels are in big trouble. Though other factors— including a perceived lack of compelling artists, artificially high CD prices, competition from "higher-value" DVDs, and the sluggish economy—are involved, file sharing has clearly had a negative impact on album sales. With the help of the Recording Industry Association of America (RIAA), the major labels shut down Napster, the first and most popular of the file-sharing websites, rather than attempt to work with the start-up to provide a pay service. (Napster, of course, reincarnated as a fee-based—and legal— service in 2003.) Though the major labels' digital distribution efforts have been ineffectual, in 2003 the RIAA began filing lawsuits against people who make major-label music files available on peer-to-peer networks. One somewhat bright spot is Apple's iTunes digital distribution website, which has been successful in selling music files owned by the majors. However, margins in digital download sales are low, so while iTunes helps Apple sell iPods, many other digital download providers are going to find it hard to stay afloat in an increasingly crowded market.

To counteract the consumer-spending slump, labels are trying to find new ways to bring in revenue. These include new contracts that entitle them to a cut of an artist's tour and merchandising revenue and an increased emphasis on placing songs in films, television shows, and—the most lucrative of all—commercials. (The video for Jewel's 2003 single "Intuition" cleverly satirized this trend while establishing her as just the kind of dance-pop idol whom advertisers would find appealing.) Legitimate music downloads and CDs packaged with bonus CDs, bonus DVDs, DualDisc formatted CDs, or fancy computer-accessible content have also helped the industry halt its downward spiral for the time being.

SPORTS

Over the past 20 or 30 years, the major trend in sports has been the tremendous growth in revenue, primed by televised broadcasting of games. This innovation led first to increased advertising sales, then to sponsorships, and then to stadium naming rights. Player endorsements provide a human (or superhuman) face to these sports marketing efforts. Over time, teams and leagues have become much more business-minded, and revenue has increased many times over. This transformation has fueled the need for business people to wheel and deal—and squeeze as much money out of every sporting event or deal as possible.

However, sports consumers (oops, make that "fans") are becoming increasingly disillusioned with the transformation of sports into a money-making machine, one that has encouraged player hubris, corporate intrusion, and a general disregard for the fans. Older fans have voted with their, um, backsides, by keeping them at home rather than seating them in stadiums. And younger people have moved toward "action" sports more to their liking, such as snowboarding and BMX, as these are exactly the kinds of things they like to do themselves.

As consumers retreat, corporate sponsors are forced to be more selective in their campaigns, usually by targeting as closely as possible the demographic they are after. They are also demanding more from sponsorship deals. Valuation services is a growing segment of sponsorship, since it attempts to quantify and evaluate the return on investment of any such deal.

A number of other trends point to possible difficulties ahead for the sports industry. The callous naming and renaming of stadiums and events has resulted in awkward and unwieldy names that have no resonance with fans. This could eventually erode fan interest, and thus have a dramatic impact on revenue. In one naming fiasco that occurred several years ago, baseball announcers in Phoenix were contractually obligated to refer to home runs as "Bank One boomers" every time the ball was hit into the stands. Chicago, on the other hand, balked at Bank One's request to attach its name to the city's football stadium. As such, in 2003, the Chicago Bears announced that Bank One would be the team's "presenting" sponsor, with all rights except that of naming the facility.

Even if stadiums had strange names though, fans could still relate to players as role models. But some prominent athletes' unsportsmanlike behavior (e.g., Latrell Sprewell's infamous on-court choking of a coach and Kobe Bryant's admission of adultery) could cause companies to start backing away from sometimes unpredictable individual athletes and focus on teams or events instead. Without that human connection, however, the sports marketing industry might take a hit.

A bright spot is the increasing popularity of sports outside of the Big Four. The previously mentioned action sports, NASCAR, and others have maintained fan interest and all areas of growth—meaning more jobs.

On the fashion front, retro seems to be in: Uniforms, athletic shoes, even Celebriducks seem to have an old-time look about them. The trend toward retro can be seen in two ways, as either the inevitable catching-up of the sports world to what the entertainment and fashion industries think is cool, or an outward sign of consumers' alienation with present-day sports and longing for a purer, simpler time.

Picking and Choosing

FIELD AND OCCUPATION

If your goal is simply to work somewhere in sports or entertainment, you might be tempted to take a shotgun approach, applying for jobs at every company in every field. Don't do it. Insiders say you'll get better results and will be happier in the long run if you concentrate on specific jobs at a select number of organizations.

First, choose the entertainment medium or sport you're most passionate about. Even if you work in accounting at a major record label, you will still eat, drink, and sleep music; someone handling group ticket sales is intimately involved with his or her team. Then focus on companies whose products you enjoy. If you're a rock fan, you probably won't want to work at a classical label. If you love hockey, NASCAR is not for you. Finally, if you have skills that can be applied in several departments, settle on a first choice. This will help you further narrow your list of prospective employers, as opportunities in departments vary from company to company.

Sports is a much more unified industry than entertainment is. Though you will probably have a smoother career path if you stick to one sport, insiders say the most important thing is experience. There are differences in, say, basketball merchandising and baseball merchandising, but the basic concepts are the same.

LOCATION

While entertainment entities are cropping up in cities across the United States and Canada, Los Angeles and New York are still the centers of film, television, and music. Any insider will tell you that, if you really want to thrive in the industry, you have to be in one of those two cities—and if it's a film job you're after, the choice is Los

Angeles. Even well-known hotbeds of independent film and music outside these centers don't have the clout or staffing levels to provide good career stepping-stones. For instance, San Francisco is a capital of independent film, but the city offers very little in the way of business-side job opportunities in that genre. You may have more responsibility at an independent outside Los Angeles or New York, but your work usually doesn't count for much if you want to move into the mainstream—what the major markets respect is major-market experience.

The sports industry is much less restricted geographically than the entertainment industry, with major-league teams in most decent-sized cities, and minor-league teams pretty much everywhere else. The governing bodies for the biggest sports tend to reside in New York, but sports agents and sports marketing companies big and small are located all over the map. So are the major sportswear companies. However, a large metropolitan area such as Los Angeles–Orange County, Dallas–Ft. Worth, or the New York area will have a higher concentration of teams and companies than a smaller city will, and therefore, more opportunities to break in and change to different employers.

SIZE

The size of the company you work for affects your career path, opportunities, and working conditions. Because the trend at entertainment conglomerates is to integrate film, television, and music resources, employees at these giant corporations may have the opportunity to move laterally between divisions—which means an expanded range of experiences and the chance to change your mind about your primary field without penalty. And, insiders say, working at a larger company is another way to expand those all-important networking possibilities. The respect given to experience at a major entertainment conglomerate is also worth considering.

For example, if you start out at a Big Four music company, then decide to switch to an independent, your major-label experience will earn you increased responsibility at the smaller company. In the reverse situation, however, your independent experience won't carry much weight at a major label. Another point in the conglomerates' favor: While entry-level compensation is in the same meager range regardless of company size, larger corporations usually offer better benefits.

On the other hand, the smaller film, television, and music companies often offer a more cohesive, less departmentalized experience than do the majors. Jobs at smaller companies tend to include a little bit of everything, while jobs at conglomerates are more sharply focused. If you're not sure which aspect of the entertainment business suits you best, the more varied work at a smaller company may help you decide. And because you're likely to take on more responsibility and face less in-house competition, the opportunity for advancement may be greater. Also, if you join a smaller company at its inception, there's always the chance it will grow in size and stature, taking you along with it on the road to influence and riches.

Nowadays, most sports teams and organizations are fairly well established, though new ventures, some flash-in-the pan, pop up frequently. Minor-league jobs will be easier to break into and may give you more exposure to a variety of job functions (including sales, in the off-season), but most people see them as a launching pad, not a destination. Major-league teams are likely where you'll need to land if you want to be able to support a family at some point.

If sports management is what you're interested in, beware of working as an assistant in a one-person agency. You may get stuck doing all of the clerical work, and the agent may be too busy to mentor you much or at all. And because most of an agent's work is done on the phone, you will likely find yourself relegated to screening calls in between all of the filing. If possible, a more established agency is probably a better place to get experience. The structure and mentoring will be useful to most lower-level employees wanting to take the leap to full-agent status. Positions in the marketing departments of companies wanting to target sports fans are reasonably plentiful, but if full-on corporate life is not for you, a smaller maker of sports clothing, equipment, or drinks may be a better way to get exposure to sports marketing while enjoying the casual small-company vibe.

The Companies

Entertainment Companies

Sports Organizations

Entertainment Companies

DREAMWORKS L.L.C.

1000 Flower Street
Glendale, CA 91201
Phone: 818-733-7000
www.dreamworks.com

DreamWorks was founded in 1994 as an "omnimedia" entertainment company, with film, music, and television arms, and, later, game software and Internet ventures. Initial expectations were high, due to the star power of the company's three major partners—acclaimed director and producer Steven Spielberg, high-powered former Disney executive Jeffrey Katzenberg, and music mogul David Geffen.

The company aimed to position itself strongly across all media, including film, music, books, games, and television. Eight years and a few false starts later, this company has produced several major hits such as the films *Saving Private Ryan*, *Shrek*, and *Catch Me If You Can* and the television show *Spin City*. DreamWorks Records developed an eclectic stable of recording artists, including the Isley Brothers, Jimmy Eat World, and Nelly Furtado, but the company sold off the division (previously headed by Geffen) to Universal Music Group in 2003, to concentrate its focus on movies and television.

The company has had several major setbacks other than the flop records and movies that plagued its early years. In 1999, the company was forced to ditch plans to build its own studios. Soon after, the company abandoned its struggling software business, DreamWorks Interactive, a joint venture with Microsoft. However, this allowed the company to right itself by focusing on traditional entertainment production, which led to major hits with blockbuster live-action movies, including two Best Picture Oscar winners—*Gladiator* and *A Beautiful Mind.* In the past few years, DreamWorks has faced other obstacles mostly due to its small size, but the lack of subsequent live-action smashes hasn't helped. On the other hand, the company's animation efforts have been wildly successful, with the *Shrek* films being the standouts. A development agreement with NBC to create *The Contender*, a boxing reality show created by Sylvester Stallone and *Survivor* creator Mark Burnett, led to some television success, but ratings for the show have been moderate.

Financial Highlights

2003 revenue: 1,250 million (est.)
1-year growth rate: –31.1 percent (est.)

Personnel Highlights

Employees: 1,100
1-year growth rate: –31.3 percent

- **Business focus:** Film and television.

- **Strengths:** Run by creative types, not suits.

- **Beware!** Largely a creative production shop, the company needs hits and block-busters to stay afloat; there are no side businesses to help it during lean times, as there are at larger companies.

- **Fact:** Microsoft's Paul Allen owns about a quarter of the company. Spielberg, Katzenberg, and Geffen own most of the rest.

EMI GROUP PLC

27 Wrights Lane
London
W8 5SW, United Kingdom
Phone:011-44-20-7795-7000
www.emigroup.com

EMI comes in last place for major-label U.S. sales, but is the third-largest music company worldwide. The company has nearly merged twice with another major—once with Warner Music Group and once with BMG Entertainment. Part of the problem may be that it's just a little too small to be a media conglomerate in its own right and a little too big to get swallowed up by another music entity. EMI has more than 70 music labels, including Capital, Virgin, Blue Note, and Real World.

The savvy that Capitol demonstrated by signing a washed-up teen idol named Frank Sinatra in the '50s and making him an icon was replicated a decade later by British EMI, which discovered the Beatles after other major labels had turned them down. In the '70s, EMI bought Blue Note, a revered jazz label, and in the '80s began aggressively reissuing its back catalogue and signing new artists, culminating in Norah Jones, who received a Grammy for Best Album of 2002. And the label that signed the Beatles also has the Stones, via Virgin Records.

In 2002, in response to its lagging market position, it completed its integration of Virgin Records (purchased in 1992) by consolidating Capitol and Virgin's noncreative departments and laying off 1,800 people. (Virgin HQ moved to New York while Capitol remains based in Hollywood, giving the company a bicoastal A&R presence.) And the company purged a quarter of its acts. In 2004, in another effort to boost its position, EMI laid off another 20 percent of its workforce (about 1,500 employees), outsourced some of its CD and DVD manufacturing, restructured some of its labels, and purged more artists to focus on its most promising acts.

Financial Highlights

2004 revenue: 3,872 million

1-year growth rate: 13.1 percent

Personnel Highlights

Employees: 7,996

1-year growth rate: 1.1 percent

- **Business focus:** Music.

- **Strengths:** Norah Jones, whose two albums have sold more than 20 million copies, has provided a much-needed boost.

- **Beware!** EMI intends to be in pretty severe cost-cutting mode for the next several years.

- **Fact:** Capitol Records was founded in 1942 by songwriting legend Johnny Mercer and two businessmen; EMI had the honor of having the Sex Pistols name a song after it.

NBC UNIVERSAL, INC.

30 Rockefeller Plaza
100 Universal City Plaza
Universal City, CA 91608
Phone: 212-644-4444
www.nbcuni.com

Formed in May 2004, NBC Universal is the result of a marriage between the National Broadcasting Company and Vivendi Universal's entertainment properties (excluding Universal Music, which was not up for sale). NBC's parent company, General Electric, owns 80 percent of the company, and Vivendi retains a 20 percent interest, which it will likely shed in the next few years.

NBC Universal's television holdings include NBC Television; Telemundo, a Spanish-language network; 29 NBC and Telemundo stations; cable channels Bravo, CNBC, MSNBC, USA Network, SCI FI Channel, TRIO; and the production company NBC Universal Television Studio. Its film holdings are grouped under Universal Pictures, including the specialty film unit, Focus Features. Finally, Universal Parks & Resorts operates its Universal Studios theme parks and other properties.

The match-up looks to be a good one. The company has already begun to repurpose and cross-promote products and should be able to negotiate better carriage deals with cable and satellite distributors.

Financial Highlights

2004 revenue: 12,886 million
1-year growth rate: −10.7 percent

Personnel Highlights

Not available.

- **Business focus:** Broadcast television and cable channels, film, film and television production, and theme parks and resorts.

- **Strengths:** GE is a conservatively run company, so NBC Universal will likely be free from the wild ups and downs that Vivendi Universal Entertainment suffered at the hands of former CEO Jean-Marie Messier.

- **Beware!** Upon the completion of the merger, insiders predict 200 to 500 layoffs will occur over the next few years, though these will most likely center on TV production jobs in the Los Angeles area.

- **Fact:** The partnership between NBC and what would become Universal Television goes back as far as September 6, 1950, when the television show *Stars Over Hollywood* premiered.

NEWS CORPORATION LIMITED

Primary U.S. Office:

1211 Avenue of the Americas
New York, NY 10036
Phone: 212-852-7059
www.newscorp.com

News Corporation Limited is one of the world's largest media companies, with diversified global operations that include film and television production; television, satellite, and cable broadcasting; and newspaper, magazine, and book publishing. News Corporation's film and television holdings are grouped under the Fox Entertainment Group, whose IPO, one of the largest in history, raised $2.8 billion in 1998.

Chairman and CEO Rupert Murdoch once said, "For better or worse, our company is a reflection of my thinking, my character, my values." Many industry observers claim that Murdoch's company has amassed much of its fortune through sleazy tabloid content and questionable business practices. Regardless, Murdoch also has an entrepreneurial spirit, which may explain why he would risk the entire company on a single venture such as B Sky B, a satellite television service.

20th Century Fox's film achievements are impressive. It has produced three of the top-performing films of all time: *Star Wars*, its *Phantom Menace* prequel, and *Titanic*. And its newest release *Star Wars: Episode III—Revenge of the Sith* broke box office records with one of the highest-grossing openings in movie history.

In 2002, it even did the unthinkable: It had film critics—the snooty kind—lauding Tom Cruise's performance in *Minority Report*. On the other hand, the earlier and unexpected success of *There's Something About Mary* has inspired other studios to focus on lower-cost teen flicks and comedies featuring midlevel stars.

Fox Broadcasting Company has come to be regarded as the fourth major broadcast network, with the help of hit programs like *The Simpsons* and *American Idol*. Though Fox is notorious for airing tabloid shows, the company is hoping to find a happy medium between riskier shows and those that appeal to a broad audience.

After much effort, News Corporation acquired 34 percent of Hughes Electronics, which owns satellite TV company DIRECTV, in 2003. (The company had lost out on an earlier bid, but reappeared when the winner, EchoStar, was prevented by antitrust officials from completing the deal.) In 2004, it sold off the money-losing Los Angles Dodgers. Also in 2004, the company moved its primary listing from Australia to the United States.

Financial Highlights

2004 revenue: 20,450 million
1-year growth rate: 1.8 percent

Personnel Highlights

Employees: 38,000
1-year growth rate: 2.7 percent

- **Business focus:** Film, television, publishing, and music.

- **Strengths:** News Corporation is a model of vertical integration.

- **Beware!** Murdoch has placed DIRECTV under the Fox umbrella, loading Fox with $4.5 billion in debt.

- **Fact:** Murdoch's wife threatened to leave him when he considered putting pictures of topless "Page 3 girls" in the *New York Post*.

SONY BMG MUSIC ENTERTAINMENT

550 Madison Avenue
New York, NY 10022
Phone: 212-833-8000
www.sonybmg.com

Many people thought that the 1999 MCA-Polygram merger, which turned the Big 6 into the Big 5, would be the last major-label marriage. After all, regulators had consistently nixed attempts by other labels to merge. But as the music industry continues to struggle with new technologies and consumer behavior, the need for cost savings is increasingly evident, and the latest merger, by Sony Music and BMG, was approved in mid-2004. The new company, Sony BMG Music Entertainment, co-owned by Sony and Bertelsmann, is expected to save as much as $80 million annually, by combining real estate, legal departments, human resources, and IT systems. (For the time being, manufacturing and music publishing are being run separately. Sony Music's operations in Japan are also excluded from the deal.) Of course, much of the savings will come from the layoff of 2,000 employees—a quarter of its staff—that took place in early 2005. The merger is expected to cost more than $300 million to complete and will largely be completed by the end of 2005.

The current line up includes Columbia Records (Bob Dylan, Dixie Chicks), Epic Records (Modest Mouse, Jennifer Lopez), RCA Music Group (Christina Aguilera, Dave Matthews Band), and Zomba Label Group, which houses the Jive (Britney Spears, Justin Timberlake) and LaFace (Outkast, Usher, Pink) labels, among others.

Sony Music chairman Andrew Lack was briefly CEO of the new entity, before becoming the first non-Japanese head of parent company Sony Corporation. On the surface, it might look as though the Sony side will be dominant. After all, Sony's 550 Madison Avenue headquarters is housing the new company, and the head honcho is a Sony man. But Clive Davis, who comes from the BMG side, has been named CEO and chairman of the North American division, so it's unlikely that he'll have to worry about any erosion of his turf. In any case, the transition for employees, even the ones who get to keep their jobs, is likely to continue for a couple years.

Financial Highlights

2004 revenue: 8,000 million (est.)
1-year growth rate: n/a

Personnel Highlights

Employees: 10,000
1-year growth rate: n/a

- **Business focus:** Music.

- **Strengths:** The pooling of Sony and BMG's artist rosters and back catalog, paired with cost savings, will help make the new company more competitive with U.S. industry leader Universal.

- **Beware!** The cultures of the two companies are very different, so friction is almost inevitable.

- **Fact:** The merger reunites Columbia Records with its former president Clive Davis, who was fired from the company amid controversy 30 years ago.

SONY CORPORATION OF AMERICA

550 Madison Avenue
New York, NY 10022
Phone: 212-833-6800
www.sony.com

Tokyo-based Sony Corporation's core business is the selling of innovative and stylish consumer electronics. However, its film and music properties, which fall under its U.S. division, have become increasingly important to the company's strategy.

Sony Pictures Entertainment houses Sony's film, home video/DVD, and television operations. Columbia TriStar Motion Picture Group is divided into four groups: Columbia; Sony Pictures Classics, which acquires independent and foreign films; Screen Gems, which focuses on films that fall in between the mass-market and art-house segments; and TriStar Pictures, which was relaunched in 2004 as a genre-based marketing and acquisitions company. Columbia TriStar Home Entertainment distributes those studios' films on video and DVD. In 2005, Sony Pictures completed its acquisition of MGM, with its valuable 4,000-strong film library.

Sony Pictures Television produces and distributes such hit shows as *Joan of Arcadia*. It has daytime television covered with the top-rated game shows *Wheel of Fortune* and *Jeopardy!* and top-rated soap operas *The Young and the Restless* and *Days of Our Lives*.

Sony owns 50 percent of Sony BMG Music Entertainment, the music group formed in 2004 as a joint venture with Bertelsmann.

Sony first entered the entertainment world in the late '80s, at the height of the Japanese economic bubble, with the purchase of CBS Records and Columbia Pictures. The latter venture started off poorly and led to disaster, after the company hired Hollywood hotshots Peter Guber and Jon Peters to run it. Something had to change, and in early 1999, new heads of Sony's U.S. divisions revealed plans to cut 17,000 jobs over 4 years, citing the need for a transition from the analog to the digital age. This proved to be a prescient move; at the time, its competitors were spending furiously in a new-media land grab that quickly turned sour. Sony focused on its core businesses instead, and the payoff came with Sony Pictures taking the top spot in box-office receipts in 2002, aided by *Spider-Man.* In fact, the plan might have worked a bit too well. In 2004 Sony announced another set of cost-cutting measures, known as "Transformation 60," that will leave it with 20,000 fewer employees by 2006—a 13 percent reduction in workforce. The plans for the entertainment businesses, which focus on convergence and cross-promotion of media, are unlikely to result in as many layoffs as the plans for the consumer electronics businesses, which will see a lot of outsourcing.

Financial Highlights

2004 revenue: $72,081 million
1-year growth rate: 13.9 percent

Personnel Highlights

Employees: 162,000
1-year growth rate: 0.0 percent

- **Business focus:** Film, television, music, game software, and consumer electronics.

- **Strengths:** Sony's conservative management style has protected the company in the past and may well do so in the future.

- **Beware!** Sony is again in cost-cutting mode.

- **Fact:** In 2005, Sir Howard Stringer, chairman and CEO of Sony Corporation of America, became the first non-Japanese head of parent company Sony Corporation.

TIME WARNER INC.

1 Time Warner Center
New York, NY 10019
Phone: 212-484-8000
www.timewarner.com

If you've ever picked up a magazine, surfed the Web, gone to a movie, or watched the news, then you've probably encountered the media behemoth that is Time Warner. The company owns a cluster of industry giants in interactive services, cable systems, publishing, cable networks, and filmed entertainment and is responsible for *Time* and *People* magazines, America Online, Warner Brothers Studios, HBO and Cinemax, and CNN.com.

The media titan made history in January 2001, when America Online completed its $106 billion merger with Time Warner to form AOL Time Warner, the biggest media deal in history to date. The company maintained efforts toward continued aggressive growth via acquisitions throughout 2001, but disappointing revenue results and over-ambitious forecasting caused it to lower initial expectations, much to the chagrin of shareholders.

Some of the company's problems have been due to the downturn in certain sectors, such as the Internet and music industries, but the America Online division—despite its position as the largest interactive online service provider in the nation—has suffered a continued decrease in stock prices (more than 50 percent since 2001) and subscribers (more than 2 million in 2003 and 2004), and has been scrutinized by the SEC and Justice Department regarding its accounting practices. In 2003, the company dropped "AOL" from its name and returned to its previous moniker.

To restore some of its former value (and luster), the corporation has moved away from growth through acquisitions to focus more closely on improving the performance of individual subsidiaries. Time Warner exited the music business in 2003 by selling off Warner Music Group to a collection of investors headed by former Universal Music executive Edgar Bronfman, Jr. It has also sold two of its sports teams, the Atlanta Hawks and the Atlanta Thrashers. In response to the company's poor performance, CEO Steve Case voluntarily stepped down in 2003 and was replaced by chairman Dick Parsons.

On a brighter note, Time Warner's movie operations are doing very well, with such assets as *The Lord of the Rings* and *The Matrix* trilogies. The studio is also responsible for high-rated television shows like *ER*.

Financial Highlights

2004 revenue: 42,089 million
1-year growth rate: 10.5 percent

Personnel Highlights

Employees: 84,900
1-year growth rate: 6.1 million

- **Business focus:** Publishing, cable television, film, and new media.

- **Strengths:** Though AOL executives have fallen from grace, the merged company still boasts an impressive ability to market entertainment via the Web.

- **Beware!** The company's low stock price still has many employees demoralized.

- **Fact:** Chairman and CEO Richard Parsons was a White House aide to Gerald Ford.

UNIVERSAL MUSIC GROUP

2220 Colorado Avenue	1755 Broadway
Santa Monica, CA 90404	New York, NY 10019
Phone: 310-865-1000	Phone: 212-841-8000

www.umusic.com

Universal Music is the largest music company in the world, created when Seagram—already the owner of MCA—acquired PolyGram in 1998. Subsidiaries include Interscope Geffen A&M, Island Def Jam Music Group, Universal Motown Records, and Verve Music Group. The restructuring that followed involved numerous cuts in staff and the artist roster.

When Vivendi, a French utility and entertainment corporation, bought Seagram in 2000, it also acquired Seagram's entertainment subsidiaries, which included Universal Studios and Universal Music Group. Its CEO at the time, Jean-Marie Messier, then went on a spending spree in a bid to consolidate Vivendi's position as a global entertainment company. Unfortunately, rising debt overtook him, and he was replaced by Jean-René Fourtou, who in 2004 sold Universal Studios, which held the film, television, and theme park properties, to General Electric, which combined those businesses with its NBC Television subsidiary, resulting in NBC Universal. The music division is not for sale at the moment, since Vivendi feels that it would be undervalued because of the down music market.

Financial Highlights

2004 revenue: 6,811 million
1-year growth rate: 9.1 percent

Personnel Highlights

Employees: 10,700

1-year growth rate: n/a

- **Business focus:** Music.

- **Strengths:** Universal Music Group is the largest of the major labels in the United States, with a deep catalog to rely on.

- **Beware!** Vivendi will most likely sell UMG after it looks like the music industry is back on track; job cuts will almost certainly follow.

- **Fact:** Chairman and CEO Doug Morris got his start in the record business as a songwriter; he wrote the Chiffons' girl-group classic "Sweet Talkin' Guy."

VIACOM INC.

1515 Broadway
New York, NY 10036
Phone: 212-258-6000
www.viacom.com

A subsidiary of National Amusement Incorporated, a large movie-theater operator, Viacom is the world's number-two entertainment conglomerate, consisting of some 18 businesses, including Paramount Pictures, MTV Networks, Nickelodeon, VH-1, Simon & Schuster publishing, Showtime Networks, and the UPN broadcast network. Viacom also owns 80 percent of Spelling Entertainment Group, which provides television programming for worldwide distribution. The company has also added CBS's broadcasting network and its King World affiliate to its list of resources, after the CBS-Viacom merger in 2000. (In 2001, the FCC made it legal for a major network to own a minor broadcast network, in this case, CBS and UPN, respectively.)

Paramount Pictures had huge box-office and home-video success with *Titanic*, in 1999, which it financed with 20th Century Fox. Other recent successes include *Saving Private Ryan*, *Braveheart*, *The Hours*, and *School of Rock*.

Viacom's greatest assets are its television properties. MTV remains the most widely distributed cable channel in the world.

The power struggle between CEO Sumner Redstone and president and COO Mel Karmazin was finally resolved when the latter left the company in 2004. The same year, Viacom decided to rid itself of its 82 percent share of Blockbuster, which has been suffering from competition from online competitors including Netflix, as well as falling prices for DVDs. (A large portion of Viacom's 2004 decline in revenue and number of employees can be attributed to the Blockbuster divestiture.)

Financial Highlights

2004 revenue: 22,526 million

1-year growth rate: –15.3 percent

Personnel Highlights

Employees: 38,350

1-year growth rate: –67.4 percent

- Business focus: Film, television, radio, and publishing.

- Strengths: MTV continues to expand beyond its cable channel base; it's now producing films and publishing books.

- Beware! Sumner Redstone is due to retire in 2007, at which time it's possible that Viacom will be split into two companies, one focused on broadcast television and radio, and the other on cable television and film.

- Fact: In World War II, Redstone was assigned to the Military Intelligence Division, where he helped break Japanese codes.

THE WALT DISNEY COMPANY

500 S. Buena Vista Street
Burbank, CA 91521
Phone: 818-560-1000
www.disney.com

Disney. The very word evokes images of childhood, magic, and America. But Disney the company has far outpaced its founder's original vision. When merger frenzy struck the media industry in the '80s and '90s, CEO Michael Eisner took a different tack. While never neglecting Disney's traditional strengths—brand, theme parks, animated feature films—he began to buy his way to the top. He started in earnest in 1993, adding Miramax Films to his expanding roster of grown-up-oriented film companies. (Another of Disney's imprints, Touchstone, had debuted in 1984, with *Splash*.) In 1995, he bought ABC as an outlet for his cartoon library and also as a means to promote his films. (He later sold the newspaper division, showing that synergy has its limits.)

Eisner now oversees the second-largest entertainment conglomerate, whose holdings include ESPN; percentages of the A&E, E!, History Channel, and Lifetime cable networks; Hollywood Pictures; Hollywood Records; Mammoth Records; as well as all sorts of other businesses with "Disney" or "Buena Vista" as part of their name.

The company has fallen on hard times in the last few years, with the slowing of the advertising market affecting television properties, the 9/11 attacks reducing travel to theme parks, and poor performance of expensive productions like *Treasure Planet* and *The Alamo* among the most damaging to the company's bottom line. The most recent blow came in early 2004, when Pixar announced that it would not renew its extremely lucrative partnership with Disney, which has resulted in such critically acclaimed animation blockbusters as *Toy Story*, *Finding Nemo*, and *The Incredibles*. Things got so bad that Roy E. Disney, Jr., the last family member on the board of directors, continually criticized Eisner in public. Eisner survived Disney's attempt to get him removed from the board (Disney was forced to retire instead, due to an age limit rule), but 45 percent of shareholders had voted against him, and he was stripped of his chairman title. He has announced that he will leave the company in 2006.

There are bright spots in the company's portfolio, however, including ABC Television's recent hit series *Lost* and *Desperate Housewives*. On the other hand, the bumpy relationship between Disney and hit machine Miramax, will come to an end in late 2005, when Miramax founders Harvey and Bob Weinstein will leave the company. Disney will retain Miramax's name and assets, but many wonder if the division will be able to maintain its course without them.

Financial Highlights

2004 revenue: 30,752 million
1-year growth rate: 13.6 percent

Personnel Highlights

Employees: 129,000
1-year growth rate: 15.2 percent

- **Business focus:** Film, television, radio, theme parks and resorts, retail, licensing, and music.

- **Strengths:** A long-standing reputation for quality and merchandising excellence—and a brand name more recognized than just about any other in the industry.

- **Beware!** Industry insiders accuse Disney of poor compensation for long hours.

- **Fact:** Disney CEO Michael Eisner began his entertainment career as an usher at NBC's studios.

WARNER MUSIC GROUP

75 Rockefeller Plaza
New York, NY 10019
Phone: 212-275-2000
www.wmg.com

"I Think We're Alone Now," a Tommy James & The Shondells recording owned by Warner Music Group, might just be an apt theme song for the company, which parent company Time Warner sold to a private investment group in 2004, for $2.6 billion.

Warner Bros. Records was founded in 1958 to issue soundtracks to Warner Brothers films. It jumped into the pop world in a big way by signing the Everly Brothers to an unprecedented $1 million dollar contract. After acquiring Frank Sinatra's Reprise label, Warner Bros. was sold a couple of times, while picking up the legendary Atlantic Recording Group and Elektra Records along the way. By the mid-'70s, the upstart company, now known as Warner Music, was vying with CBS Records for the top slot in the music industry. By the early '90s, however, the label's market share was slipping, so in 1999 a merger with the similarly beleaguered EMI was proposed, only to be nixed by European regulators.

In 2004, a group of investors, of whom the most prominent was former Seagram and Universal executive Edgar Bronfman, Jr., bought Warner Music Group from Time Warner. Bronfman was installed as chairman and CEO. Lyor Cohen was poached from Universal Music Group to serve as head of the U.S. operation; Jason Flom was put in charge of the newly formed Atlantic Records Group, which contains the Atlantic, Elektra, and Lava labels; and Tom Whalley was put in charge of Warner Bros. Records, which includes the Reprise, Sire, Nonesuch, Maverick, Warner Nashville, and Word labels. Other divisions of WMG include Warner Strategic Marketing (home of the Rhino label), WEA Distribution, and Warner-Chappell Music Publishing. Bronfman immediately cut 1,000 jobs in early 2004. In May 2005, WMG's new owners' attempt to take the company flopped, when the original asking price of $24 a share was deemed overinflated and its biggest-selling act, Linkin Park, criticized the IPO as being in the interest of the label's owners and no one else. On the first day of trading, the stock price had dropped to a mere $16.40.

Financial Highlights

2004 revenue: 2,548 million
1-year growth rate: −24.5 percent

Personnel Highlights

Employees: 4,000
1-year growth rate: −4.8 percent

- **Business focus:** Music.

- **Strengths:** WMG has a seasoned group of music executives running the company.

- **Beware!** Employee morale is quite low, due to recent layoffs, the company's shaky IPO, and general uncertainty about the company's future.

- **Fact:** Chairman Edgar Bronfman, Jr., was not only heir to the Seagram's family fortune but also a semi-successful songwriter before joining the family business.

Sports Organizations

ADIDAS-SALOMON AG

Primary U.S. office:
5055 N. Greeley Avenue
Portland, OR 97217
Phone: 971-234-2300
www.adidas-salomon.com

The Adidas brand, which has been around since the 1940s, continues to dominate the athletic shoe industry, right behind Nike. In an effort to expand beyond its traditional niche, Adidas acquired Salomon, a French sporting goods manufacturer, for $1.4 billion in 1997. The merger effectively expanded Adidas' reach beyond sports shoes to encompass ski, tennis, cycling, and golf equipment; swimwear; bicycle components; and equipment for team sports such as basketball and soccer.

Chairman and CEO Robert Louis-Dreyfus brought the company back from the brink of bankruptcy in 1993 by redirecting capital toward advertising and moving production to Asia. The company has slowly gained ground since then, despite some disappointing returns, particularly from its Salomon golf subsidiary Taylor Made Golf. Louis-Dreyfus retired in 2001 and was replaced by former COO Herbert Hainer.

In 2001, the company launched a leisure-wear line aimed at teen consumers, its core market. In recent years, it has also opened retail outlets in several countries, to gain visibility with consumers and to help differentiate itself from its non-Nike competitors. In 2004, the company acquired Valley Apparel Company, which makes professional and collegiate sportswear. In 2005, the company launched a new line of women's sportswear designed by fashion designer Stella McCartney, daughter of Paul and Linda McCartney.

Financial Highlights

2004 revenue: 8,134 million

1-year growth rate: 3.4 percent

Personnel Highlights

Employees: 17,000

1-year growth rate: 8.4 percent

- **Business focus:** Sports and leisure wear, athletic equipment, and retail.

- **Strengths:** Making strategic acquisitions to stay ahead of most of its rivals.

- **Beware!** Company's shares were delisted from the Paris stock exchange in 2003; it remains on the German exchange.

- **Fact:** In 1984, turned down Michael Jordan for an endorsement deal. He went on to ensure Nike's dominance.

THE GATORADE COMPANY

555 W. Monroe Street
Chicago, IL 60661-3605
Phone: 312-222-7111
www.gatorade.com

Thirsty for a career in sports marketing? Gatorade may be able to satisfy that craving. With $2 billion in annual sales, it dominates the sports-drink market, and is the official sports drink of the MLB, NBA, NFL, U.S. Soccer, WNBA, and numerous other leagues, teams, and events.

The company got its start in the mid-'60s, when a group of doctors at the University of Florida concocted a beverage that would help their ailing football team, the Gators, who were performing badly due to the oppressive Florida heat. The drink worked wonders on their performance and became so popular that a company was formed to meet increasing demand. The company had several owners before becoming a co-subsidiary of PepsiCo, paired with Tropicana.

Though Gatorade has always been keen to market its wares to athletes and sports fans via endorsements and sponsorships, it formally entered the big leagues of advertising when it created a television commercial, starring Michael Jordan, for the 2003 Super Bowl. Current endorsees include Yao Ming, Mia Hamm, and Derek Jeter.

Financial Highlights

2004 revenue: 183 million (est.)
1-year growth rate: n/a

Personnel Highlights

Employees: 1,440

1-year growth rate: n/a

- **Business focus:** Sports drinks.

- **Strengths:** Gatorade is firmly backed by years of scientific research, and the Gatorade Sports Science Institute is a leader in sports-nutrition research.

- **Beware!** As the drink market becomes more sophisticated, Gatorade may be vulnerable to brands with a hipper cachet.

- **Fact:** Gatorade was named after the Florida Gators football team.

HOST COMMUNICATIONS, INC.

546 East Main Street
Lexington, KY 40508
Phone: 859-226-4678
www.hostcommunications.com

Bull Run is the holding company for Host Communications, a marketing company focusing on college sports. It also has a 37 percent stake in iHigh, a sports marketing company focusing on high schools. Host, named one of the top-five sports marketing companies by *SportsBusiness Journal*, has become the focus of Bull Run since being acquired in 1999.

The National Tour Association has been a client of Host since 1974, and Host began its relationship with the NCAA the following year, when it was granted radio rights to NCAA games. Host's involvement with the NCAA has expanded over the years to include publishing, TV, radio, and interactive media production, and corporate marketing representation.

Host also made inroads into professional sports with affinity-event initiatives such as NBA Hoop-It-Up and the "got milk? 3v3 Soccer Shootout" (Major League Soccer), but in 2004 decided to exit the events business due to poor performance, which resulted in a reduction in both revenues and number of employees.

Financial Highlights

2004 revenue: 56 million
1-year growth rate: −33.4

Personnel Highlights

Employees: 275

1-year growth rate: 27.6 percent

- **Business focus:** Sports and affinity marketing and production services.

- **Strengths:** Very strong in the college market.

- **Beware!** The company may have overextended itself; in 2002, Host had to renegotiate an 11-year, $575 million deal with CBS Sports after the company realized it couldn't afford to honor the contract.

- **Fact:** Bull Run used to be in the business of making computer printers.

IMG

1360 E. 9th Street, Suite 100
Cleveland, OH 44114
Phone: 216-522-1200
www.imgworld.com

With nearly 3,000 employees in 30 countries, IMG (formerly called International Marketing Group) is the largest sports marketing and management company in the world.

The company—and indeed the industry—traces its roots to a legendary 1960 hand-shake deal between founder, chairman, and golf-enthusiast Mark H. McCormack and golfer Arnold Palmer for McCormack to take care of Palmer's finances. He did that and more, brokering endorsement and licensing deals to swell his client's bank account. He was so successful that he started representing other athletes, and soon began a television arm to produce sports programming. Now, IMG is involved with almost every facet of sports marketing: It creates proprietary sports events, coordinates the participants, the sponsors, and the broadcast outlets, and takes a bite out of each piece of pie.

IMG gets involved early on in an athlete's career, even providing sports-training facilities for its athletes. It signs the most promising to management contracts early on and then grooms them for later success. Clients include Tiger Woods, Serena and Venus Williams, and the International Olympic Committee.

Founder and visionary McCormack died in 2003. In 2004, IMG shuttered its artists division and was bought by buyout company Forstmann Little & Co.

Financial Highlights

2003 revenue: 1,200 million (est.)
1-year growth rate: –7.7 percent (est.)

Personnel Highlights

Employees: 2,200

1-year growth rate: –26.7 percent

- **Business focus:** Sports marketing, management, event planning, and television production.

- **Strengths:** Vertically integrated and independent, and thus better equipped to handle economic downturns than competitors owned by large advertising companies.

- **Beware!** Since the death of its founder and subsequent sale, the future of IMG is very uncertain.

- **Fact:** IMG created the '80s television show *Battle of the Network Stars*.

MAJOR LEAGUE BASEBALL

245 Park Avenue
New York, NY 10167
Phone: 212-931-7800
www.mlb.com

Major League Baseball (MLB) is made up of 30 separate franchises that operate as individual businesses—the association is run through revenue-sharing provided by payroll and luxury taxes. Commissioner Bud Selig has been given great authority to distribute wealth among the teams, block trades, and determine fines, among other issues.

Baseball has recovered spectacularly from the devastating players' strike of 1994, thanks partly to Mark McGwire and Sammy Sosa's race to break Roger Maris's home-run record during the 1998 season. However, a trend toward corporate ownership of teams raises questions about fan loyalty.

In 2004, MLB bowed to longstanding pressure to install policies require testing for performance-enhancing drug use. Also, the nearly averted strike of 2002 embarrassed officials and disgusted fans. Under Selig's management, however, MLB is pulling together to try to right its course. For example, in 2004, it signed a $650 million deal with XM Radio.

Financial Highlights

2004 revenue: 4,100 million (est.)
1-year growth rate: 7.9 percent

Personnel Highlights

Not available.

- **Business focus:** Professional sports.

- **Strengths:** MLB scored a $2.5 billion deal giving Fox exclusive rights to air all postseason games through the 2006 season, thus helping its bottom line considerably.

- **Beware!** Even if MLB overcomes its recent image problems, it will still have to deal with a younger demographic raised on basketball, soccer, NASCAR, and extreme sports.

- **Fact:** MLB plans to cut two teams by 2006.

NATIONAL ASSOCIATION FOR STOCK CAR AUTO RACING, INC.

1801 W. International Speedway Boulevard
Daytona Beach, FL 32115
Phone: 386-253-0611
www.nascar.com

The National Association for Stock Car Auto Racing (NASCAR) is a closely held, family-led company that runs and sanctions auto races throughout the United States. In the 1990s, NASCAR succeeded in expanding the sport's appeal and revenues, as well as the geographic location of the races. Once confined to the southeastern United States and a predominantly white male audience, its events are now widely attended by a more varied crowd, and 17 of the top 20 sporting events in 1998 were NASCAR races. The only other professional sport with stronger fan support—and television ratings—is pro football.

The company has increased its merchandising efforts and continues to hold onto large sponsors, such as Craftsman and Busch. However R.J. Reynolds recently announced it would no longer sponsor the Winston Cup race, which had lauded the tobacco company's name since 1971. NASCAR-emblazoned T-shirts, caps, and model cars are available on the official website, and even more items have recently become available on eBay. The official NASCAR website is owned and operated by Turner Sports Interactive, a division of Time Warner.

With continually increasing television ratings for NASCAR races, things look good for the association—and its sponsors.

Financial Highlights

2002 revenue: 3,400 million (est.)
1-year growth rate: n/a

Personnel Highlights

Employees: 450

1-year growth rate: n/a

- **Business focus:** Professional sports.

- **Strengths:** As a family-owned company, NASCAR is largely immune to the ups and downs of the stock market.

- **Beware!** On the other hand, family-run companies are not known for letting outsiders run things, if that's your ambition.

- **Fact:** In what is surely a sign of NASCAR's growing respectability, cellular phone company Nextel has replaced R.J. Reynolds (maker of cigarettes, among other things) as the title sponsor of the Winston Cup series, starting in 2004.

NATIONAL BASKETBALL ASSOCIATION

Olympic Tower
645 Fifth Avenue
New York, NY 10022
Phone: 212-407-8000
www.nba.com

Despite a shaky adolescence, the National Basketball Association (NBA), formed in 1949, has grown to become the third-largest sports league in the United States. It wasn't until the 1980s that the popularity of the sport finally took off, but it has since grown by leaps and bounds. With NBA teams now located in Canada, and new franchises forming in the Women's Basketball Association, the league is ever expanding.

Growth is also due in part to increased revenue from marketing, apparel licensing (team shirts and caps), sporting goods, trading cards, magazines, home videos, toys, video games, and collectibles. The NBA currently has 150 licensees that manufacture and sell consumer apparel and other goods with the NBA logo or team logos. In 1998, the NBA joined with The Rank Group to open up a chain of Hard Rock cafes, and in 1999 began a 24-hour basketball network.

NBC was recently outbid in its television contract with the NBA by ESPN and Turner Networks (owned by Walt Disney and Time Warner, respectively), whose offer of $4.6 billion dwarfed NBC's $1.3 billion offer. This ended up putting the majority of playoff games on cable channels, which irritated many fans. The NBA earned itself another (figurative) black eye in 2004, when a brawl erupted between players and fans at an Indiana Pacers/Detroit Pistons game. The incident resulted in criminal charges being filed against participants on both sides, and greatly disappointed fans who felt that players have largely failed as role models.

Financial Highlights

2004 revenue: 3,000 million (est.)

1-year growth rate: n/a

Personnel Highlights

Not available.

- **Business focus:** Professional sports.

- **Strengths:** In Yao Ming, the NBA has finally found a popular, charming, talented, and squeaky-clean replacement for poster-boy Michael Jordan, who retired in 2003.

- **Beware!** If the majority of games are televised on cable, as was the case for the 2002–03 season, many fans will not be able to see them.

- **Fact:** Robert Johnson, the man behind the BET network, is the first African-American to own a basketball team, the Charlotte Bobcats.

NATIONAL FOOTBALL LEAGUE INC.

280 Park Avenue
New York, NY 10017
Phone: 212-450-2000
www.nfl.com

The National Football League (NFL), whose commissioner is Paul Tagliabue, is a trade association for 32 teams in the United States. The NFL's purpose is to promote the sport, develop new opportunities, license the team logos, and, most important, collect dues and royalties from the franchises. The league formed in 1920 as the American Football Association; in 1922 it made the change to its current name.

In 1966, the NFL merged with its rival, the American Football League. The Super Bowl soon followed, generating high television advertising revenues over the years. NFL International was founded in 1996 and has offices in Frankfurt, London, Mexico City, Tokyo, and Toronto.

In 1998, the NFL secured an 8-year package of television deals worth a whopping $18.6 billion, and in 2004 extended the deal to 2011, for an additional $8 billion. The NFL has a separate deal with DIRECTV, worth $3.5 billion, that allows subscribers to watch their choice of Sunday games. In 2002–03, the NFL reorganized its conferences to make more geographic sense. The sport suffered some bad press in 2004, as a result of Janet Jackson exposing her breast during the Super Bowl, but as far as sports scandals go, it's nothing compared to what baseball, hockey, or basketball have suffered recently.

Financial Highlights

2004 revenue: 6,000 million (est.)
1-year growth rate: 9.1 percent (est.)

Personnel Highlights

Employees: 450

1-year growth rate: 0.0 percent

- **Business focus:** Professional sports.

- **Strengths:** Excellent TV deals, worth more almost $30 billion.

- **Beware!** Though the picture is very rosy for the NFL right now, NASCAR is nipping at its heels.

- **Fact:** Football is the most popular televised pro sport.

NATIONAL HOCKEY LEAGUE

1251 Avenue of the Americas, 47th Floor
New York, NY 10020
Phone: 212-789-2000
www.nhl.com

The National Hockey League (NHL) dates back to 1917, when the league had four teams and a 22-game schedule. Today, the league includes 30 teams in the United States and Canada as well as various minor-league and semipro teams. Since the 1990s, the league has grown, especially under the leadership of Commissioner Gary Bettman.

New rules that make the game quicker and easier to follow have helped attendance increase each season. In 1994, a player lockout failed and hurt attendance in the major franchises. In 1997, the league announced four new expansions: Atlanta and Nashville in 1997, and in 2000 and 2001, Columbus, Ohio, and Minnesota.

The NHL is currently in the middle of a major crisis. The league lost $500 million between 2002 and 2005, due largely to the cancellation of the 2004–05 season because of a dispute between owners and players over a proposed salary cap for players. (As much as 70 percent of revenue goes toward player salaries.) This can't go on, of course, and in March 2005, Bain Capital Partners and Game Plan International offered to buy the entire league for $3.5 billion. This is unlikely to fly, since all 30 owners would have to agree, and since it somewhat undervalues the league, but the fact that anyone would even make such an offer illustrates how troubled the sport is.

Financial Highlights

2004 revenue: 2,100 million
1-year growth rate: 5.2 percent

Personnel Highlights

Not available.

- **Business focus:** Professional sports.

- **Strengths:** Recent changes to scoring rules have stepped up the sport's pace.

- **Beware!** The cancellation of the 2004–05 season leaves the league severely weakened and the future of the sport in question.

- **Fact:** Hockey is the national sport of Canada.

NEW BALANCE ATHLETIC SHOE, INC.

Brighton Landing
20 Guest Street
Boston, MA 02135
Phone: 617-783-4000
www.newbalance.com

In the crowded field of athletic footwear, fourth-largest sports shoe manufacturer New Balance has chosen to be a workhorse, rather than the show horses that competitors Nike and Adidas-Salomon so clearly are. Rather than developing bleeding-edge styles for Tokyo teens, the company "remains committed to fit over fashion and the belief that shoes that fit better, perform better." Other philosophies include keeping at least some U.S. manufacturing, making shoes in a range of widths, and avoiding costly high-profile endorsers.

The company must be doing something right. After all, 800-pound gorilla Nike has taken a page from New Balance's book by emphasizing function over fashion and lowering prices. This long-term approach could play well to consumers who are starting to become alienated by the big-corporation nature of much of the sports world.

New Balance traces its origins to an arch-support company founded in 1906 by William J. Riley. He sold the company to his daughter and son-in-law, Eleanor and Paul Kidd, in 1954. It wasn't until 1961 that they brought out the Trackster, an innovative running shoe, with little fanfare but spectacular word-of-mouth success. The Kidds sold the company in 1972 to chairman and CEO Jim Davis, who has continued to uphold New Balance's no-nonsense approach to product development and marketing.

In late 2003, the company announced a partnership with a children's apparel maker Franco Apparel to create a full line of NB wear for infants and kids. In early 2004, it acquired Warrior Lacrosse, a manufacturer of high-performance lacrosse footwear and apparel. With these purchases, the company is hoping to broaden its customer base to include younger people, especially in Europe. New Balance announced a plan to increase European sales fivefold, to capitalize on the brand's growing popularity in that market.

Financial Highlights

2003 revenue: 1,200 million (est.)

1-year growth rate: 0.0 percent (est.)

Personnel Highlights

Employees: 2,600

1-year growth rate: 8.3 percent

- **Business focus:** Athletic shoes and sportswear.

- **Strengths:** Smart management has kept the company competitive with its much bigger rivals.

- **Beware!** As a smaller player, it is less able to weather downturns.

- **Fact:** For decades, the company's bread and butter consisted of arch supports and prescription footwear.

NIKE, INC.

1 Bowerman Drive
Beaverton, OR 97005
Phone: 503-671-6453
www.nike.com

Nike sits on top of the shoe world. Among other things, it controls roughly 40 percent of the U.S. athletic shoe market. The company famous for its "Just Do It" tagline has expanded its reach to include subsidiaries such as Cole Haan shoes and apparel, Nike Team Sports (hats), and Bauer Nike Hockey. Separate business units within Nike include The Jordan/Jumpman 23 brand and Nike Golf. The image-conscious company has 18,000 retail locations, including Niketown and Nikewomen stores, all over the United States and in 140 countries.

A keen ability to anticipate trends, popular celebrity-athlete endorsements, an aggressive advertising style, and cheap third-world manufacturing (which got it into hot water for a time with allegations of human rights violations) have kept Nike ahead of the pack—despite the rise of midpriced shoe competitors such as Skechers. In recent years, the company has been focusing on direct sales via its Niketown stores and e-tailing site. To that end, in 2001, Nike opened its first Nikewomen (formerly Nikegoddess) store in California, which caters to a female clientele. Also that year, the company announced the launching of its Tiger Woods' apparel line for Nordstrom, as well as its first line of Nike golf clubs.

In 2002, Nike took over Hurley International, a premium teen-lifestyle brand, and in September 2003, it acquired the ailing Converse, maker of the classic "Chuck Taylor" basketball shoes, in an attempt to trump Adida's entry into the retro niche market. In 2004, it bought athletic apparel and shoemaker Official Starter, for which it has announced plans to rename Exeter Brands Group focusing on creating products for discount stores such as Target and Wal-Mart. In 2005, the company for the first time released information on its overseas suppliers, so that critics can finally verify the company's claims of corporate responsibility in factories in third-world countries.

Financial Highlights

2004 revenue: 12,253 million
1-year growth rate: 14.5 percent

Personnel Highlights

Employees: 24,667
1-year growth rate: 5.9 percent

- **Business focus:** Athletic shoes, sportswear, and retail.

- **Strengths:** Sheer size and marketing ability.

- **Beware!** Customer fickleness in Asia resulted in job cuts in 1998; this scenario could repeat itself.

- **Fact:** Chairman, CEO, and cofounder Phil Knight owns more than 80 percent of the company.

OCTAGON WORLDWIDE INC.

1270 Avenue of the Americas, 7th Floor
New York, NY 10020
Phone: 212-597-8170
www.octagon.com

Octagon Worldwide is one of the world's largest sports marketing companies, and also one of the newest. Whereas competitor IMG was created with an athlete-centered approach, Octagon was created from more of a corporate-branding perspective. Formed in 1997 and launched globally in 1999 by Interpublic, the advertising conglomerate, Octagon set about taking advantage of the exploding world of sponsorship and sports marketing. Technically, the company falls under the Interpublic Group of Companies, Inc. Octagon's subsidiaries include Octagon Motorsports and Octagon CSI, which focuses on televised sports production and distribution. Octagon also handles sponsorships, facilities representation, event management, and merchandising and licensing.

Octagon represents Mike Vick, Kazuhisa Ishii, and Anna Kournikova, among others.

Financial Highlights

Not available.

Personnel Highlights

Employees: 1,500 (est.)
1-year growth rate: n/a

- **Business focus:** Sports marketing, management, event planning, and television production.

- **Strengths:** Its relationships with other Interpublic companies gives it an advantage in executing advertising campaigns and in sourcing corporate deals.

- **Beware!** Parent company Interpublic's serious financial and legal woes may affect Octagon and other sister companies; rumors of layoffs at Octagon are rife.

- **Fact:** The company was able to launch quickly by inducing executives from competitors to jump ship.

REEBOK INTERNATIONAL LTD.

1895 J. W. Foster Boulevard
Canton, MA 02021
Phone: 781-401-5000
www.reebok.com

Though the name Reebok seems to scream "'80s!" it has the longest history of any major shoe manufacturer. Reebok traces its origins to a spiked running shoe created in the late 1800s. J. W. Foster's shoe was so popular that he created a company, named after himself, to market it. In the late 1950s, two of his grandsons founded a sister company, named Reebok, which later absorbed the original company. Things got interesting in 1979, when an American named Paul Fireman took notice of Reebok and set himself up as the North American distributor. Reebok USA soon found a niche in the exploding aerobic-footwear market, and grew quickly throughout the 1980s. The company got on the "step" bandwagon early and created a product line around that fitness craze.

By the early '90s, Reebok felt ready to move in on Nike's preeminence in the sports market, and signed up Shaquille O'Neal, Allen Iverson, and Venus Williams as sponsors. The company lost much of its market share in the '90s, however, and by decade's end had announced layoffs of 20 percent of its staff. Soon after, Reebok got into the uniform business, providing uniforms to the NBA and the WNBA, as well as the NFL. In 2002, it unveiled Rbk, an attempt to woo the urban market with a fashion-conscious approach, with rapper Jay-Z as one of the pitchmen. In 2004, the company purchased the Canadian-based Hockey Co., in an effort to expand its uniform and equipment business, and in 2005, it announced an ambitious celebrity-driven ad campaign entitled "I Am What I Am."

Financial Highlights

2004 revenue: 3,785 million

1-year growth rate: 8.6 percent

Personnel Highlights

Employees: 9,102

1-year growth rate: 17.3 percent

- **Business focus:** Athletic shoes, sportswear, and team uniforms.

- **Strengths:** Revitalized strategy after years in the doldrums.

- **Beware!** Reebok is currently pursuing glitzy urban credibility at a time when the other manufacturers are pursuing a retro strategy. Is it still behind the times?

- **Fact:** During the mid-'80s aerobics boom Reebok was briefly the number-one shoe manufacturer.

SFX SPORTS GROUP, INC.

5335 Wisconsin Avenue NW
Suite 850
Washington, DC 20015
Phone: 202-686-2000
www.sfxsports.com

People love to hate Clear Channel, but the company has one subsidiary that would raise the ire of no one. SFX Sports Group began when SFX Entertainment, a live-entertainment company, bought FAME, a sports marketing and management company, in 1998. SFX bought more sports-related companies in 1999 and bundled them together as SFX Sports the same year. In 2000, radio and live-entertainment giant Clear Channel purchased SFX, which then continued to snap up sports companies. It is now an independently run subsidiary of Clear Channel Entertainment, the live-entertainment branch of Clear Channel.

Though dwarfed by Clear Channel's radio, live-event, and billboard businesses, the sports management division is growing. It has ten offices in the United States and several offices in Europe and Australia. Clients include Jerry Rice, Andre Agassi, and Andy Roddick.

Financial Highlights

Not available.

Personnel Highlights

Not available.

- **Business focus:** Sports management and marketing.

- **Strengths:** Clear Channel's dominance in radio and live events means that SFX can offer clients built-in marketing channels.

- **Beware!** As a small business outside of Clear Channel's main focus, SFX Sports could be the first to go in a corporate shake-up.

- **Fact:** SFX doesn't really stand for anything; it's just now-departed founder Robert F. X. Sillerman's final three initials jumbled up.

On the Job

The Big Picture: Entertainment

Production Assistant

Executive Assistant

Development Executive

Publicity Coordinator

The Big Picture: Sports

Director of Sponsorships

Media Relations Assistant

Athlete Coordinator

The Big Picture: Entertainment

Here's a sampling of positions in different departments and companies in film, music, and television.

Note that marketing and publicity positions vary a lot among companies. In addition to those listed below, jobs range from assistant in postproduction marketing and creative advertising, to director of home entertainment marketing, to marketing coordinator for the interactive division. Marketing jobs connected with websites are also available, and they're a good place to start for those with experience in new media but none in entertainment. The Internet and other new technologies used in producing and marketing entertainment products also mean there are many opportunities for skilled tech types in the industry.

Finally, assistantships exist in almost every department of entertainment companies, even if they're not mentioned here.

ACQUISITIONS DEPARTMENT

The acquisitions department buys products for distribution—television show episodes made by television production companies, for example, or CDs produced by independent record labels.

Acquisitions Assistant

Supports the senior staff of business affairs and acquisitions. An acquisitions assistant is entry level or has a year of experience in acquisitions. This is a training spot for executives—lucky go-getters eventually move from here up the rungs to vice president positions.

Salary range: low $20,000s to $30,000

Vice President of Acquisitions/International Acquisitions

Researches prospective properties from domestic or international markets. Duties may include screening films for distribution and reading scripts for production. Acquisitions VPs generally have 3 to 5 years of experience in entertainment. Law degrees are highly encouraged in this department.

Salary range: $60,000 to $70,000s

ARTISTS & REPERTOIRE

A&R Executive

Finds the talent for the record company to produce. The position requires going to lots of concerts and helping negotiate contracts. While most people in this position have college degrees, in the end what it takes to succeed are an ear for talent, trend-spotting ability, and luck.

Salary range: $40,000 to much, much more

BUSINESS AND LEGAL AFFAIRS DEPARTMENT

Attorney

Handles artist contracts and general legal affairs for the corporate division. One to 2 years of entertainment law experience is preferred.

Salary range: $40,000s

Senior Attorney

Oversees general legal affairs for the corporate division and negotiates terms for acquisitions. Senior attorneys have 5 or more years of entertainment law experience.

Salary range: around $100,000

HOME VIDEO DEPARTMENT

Customer Service Representative

Handles customer inquiries. Representatives are entry level, but previous video retail experience is preferred.

Salary range: $20,000s

Regional Sales Representative

Sells home products such as DVDs and videotapes to retail stores. Regional sales representatives have several years of entertainment sales experience.

Salary range: Base salary plus commission can go up into the $70,000s.

INTERNATIONAL DEPARTMENT

International Operations Executive

Handles contracts with foreign distributors and oversees contracts for domestic distribution of foreign properties. A law degree and entertainment law experience are often required.

Salary range: $60,000 to $70,000s

International Sales Executive

Monitors sales of products such as DVDs, CDs, and videotapes in international markets. Several years of entertainment sales experience are usually required.

Salary range: $60,000 to $70,000s

FILM COMPANY MUSIC DEPARTMENT

Manager of Music and Soundtracks

Finds appropriate music for films. Senior music managers have experience at record labels.

Salary range: $40,000 and up

PRODUCTION DEPARTMENT

Creative Executive

Heads up the development department; solicits new scripts and develops existing scripts for production. Creative executives spend most of their time dealing with writers.

Salary range: $30,000 to $50,000

Vice President of Production

Responsibilities range from getting projects started (purchasing scripts and so on) to overseeing actual production. Production VPs have 3 to 5 years of production experience.

Salary range: $75,000 to $100,000

Music Producer

Works with musical artists in the recording studio to define and hone their sound and songs.

Salary range: $30,000 to $80,000

Production Coordinator

Manages the nitty-gritty details of television or film production, setting shooting schedules, arranging for permits needed to shoot on location, managing production assistants, and so on. Usually requires PA (production assistant) experience.

Salary range: $30,000 to $50,000s

PUBLICITY DEPARTMENT

Publicity Assistant

Supports the vice president of corporate public relations. Tasks are generally administrative. Publicity assistants are entry level, but companies prefer a year of experience.

Salary range: $20,000s

Vice President of Field Publicity

Oversees promotional tours publicizing company properties. Field publicity VPs have 5 or more years of publicity experience, preferably in the entertainment industry.

Salary range: $80,000 to $100,000

Vice President of Corporate Public Relations

Manages the company's brand or image. Duties include fielding questions from the press, writing press releases, monitoring coverage of the company, and writing speeches for senior executives. Corporate PR VPs have 5 or more years of public relations experience, preferably in the entertainment field.

Salary range: $80,000 to $100,000

SERVICING DEPARTMENT

Servicing Manager

Oversees postproduction work, such as sound and film editing. Servicing managers have 3 to 5 years of experience in postproduction.

Salary range: $40,000s

TALENT AGENCY

Agent

Represents talent—writers, actors, directors, musicians—and finds work for the talent, negotiating contracts and earning a percentage of what the talent is paid for projects. Also sometimes provides personal financial management. Requires a college degree along with industry and negotiating savvy.

Salary range: $30,000 to $100,000 and up

Reader

Reads and provides coverage of books and scripts to find new writing clients for the agency to represent and to evaluate new projects for agency talent.

Salary range: $25,000 to $40,000

THEATRICAL DISTRIBUTION DEPARTMENT

Vice President of Theatrical Distribution

Manages domestic film distribution. Distribution VPs have 3 to 5 years of entertainment distribution experience.

Salary range: $70,000s

THEATRICAL MARKETING DEPARTMENT

Vice President of Theatrical Marketing

Determines methods and budgets for marketing films for theatrical release. Previous entertainment marketing experience is required.

Salary range: $70,000s

TELEVISION DEPARTMENT

Vice President of Television

Searches for properties (television movies, pilots, previously aired shows, films) for distribution; screens prospective properties. Television VPs have entertainment distribution experience.

Salary range: $70,000s

Production Assistant

PAs, as they're commonly called, are entry-level staffers at movie studio offices and on film and television production crews. Because these jobs involve long hours, meager pay, and gross amounts of pride-swallowing, you might think there's not much competition for them. You'd be wrong. To make matters worse, the number of positions is so limited that PAs often start as unpaid interns. And you're expected to accept all this with a big perky smile on your face. But if you do, and you excel at the work, you're likely to start moving up in the movie or television industry.

THE WORK

The Butler meets The Secretary meets The Handyman: That's probably the best way to describe in a nutshell what being a PA is like. The PA's responsibilities consist mainly of clerical and gofer work. If you have an aversion to answering phones, photocopying scripts, and making coffee, you'd best find another occupation. A PA's work is as varied as the hours are long. The mix of tasks depends on your place of employment—for example, a position on a television or film production crew will most likely include some manual labor. ("No, we need the stack of hay bales over there on the other side of the pickup truck," the director might say, looking around for PAs.) Although the work may be tedious, it does educate you on how the business works. As an insider says, "You're doing brainless work, but if you listen to the conversations around you, you can learn how to get a production running. And you can do a lot of networking. You will interface with people on both the corporate and creative sides of the industry on a daily basis." The relationships you form while a PA often determine how long you stay at the bottom. While one PA may become an executive assistant within a matter of months, another may spend half a decade in the position. For the most part, though, PAs move up on the chain of command within a year or two.

SAMPLE PROJECT

The producer needs to sign an A-list actor for the lead role in his latest project. Your job is to photocopy the script and deliver it to the home of Hollywood's biggest star. The clock reads 4:45, and the script needs to be there by 5:30. It's Friday, so the 405 Freeway has been gridlocked since noon. You'll have to negotiate Hollywood's back streets to arrive in Malibu from Culver City in 45 minutes. And, oh yeah—on the way back, you'll need to stop in Santa Monica to pick up some of that coffee everybody in the office loves.

A DAY IN THE LIFE OF A PRODUCTION ASSISTANT

6:30   Punch the snooze button a couple of times before climbing out of bed.

8:00   Arrive at the producer's office on the studio lot. Check e-mail and voice mail, then skim the trade papers until everyone else arrives.

9:00   Make photocopies of scripts your producer is thinking about optioning.

10:00   The development executives start receiving calls from agents about projects the production company might be interested in. Between rings, dream about the day they'll be calling for you.

11:30   Sort and deliver mail.

12:00   An agent across town has a hot new script. Drive over to pick it up, fighting traffic on the 10. On the way back, grab lunch from an In-N-Out Burger drive-through window.

1:00   While eating, start reading another screenplay nobody else wants to read. Your coverage of it is due at the end of the day.

4:15   Time to make the bank deposits. Head out to your car—and as you walk out the door, realize that the producer is discussing an upcoming project with Gwyneth Paltrow. Think to yourself, She'd be perfect for the lead in my movie.

5:15   Back at the office, watch the dailies from the company's newest film in production, a fish-out-of-water romantic comedy.

5:30   Complete your coverage, explaining why a family comedy about a serial killer will never work.

6:15   Finish reading the trade papers.

6:45   Go home.

Executive Assistant

If you begin as an intern or production assistant and persevere, you will eventually graduate to the position of executive assistant—and newcomers with work experience may qualify for an assistantship right off the bat. Assistant positions exist in a number of departments at every entertainment company.

THE WORK

Like PA work, an executive assistant's work at a film studio, television network, or record label is largely clerical. "When I worked as a junior assistant to the president and VP of the legal department, I was essentially a receptionist," one insider says. Responsibilities include answering calls, sorting mail, and following trends. People with degrees from the country's best colleges may feel that this sort of work is below them. No matter—assistantships are the training ground for executive positions, and at the most successful companies they're often filled by people with MBAs and law degrees.

Unlike a PA, an executive assistant is in a powerful position. "You're the first filter," an insider says, referring to the fact that the assistant makes critical decisions as to who gets to talk to the executive. Another plus is that many executives mentor their assistants. And since the industry is so changeable, you never know when you'll make the crucial jump from being an assistant to having one.

Savvy assistants looking to move ahead seek out opportunities to provide extra coverage on scripts, pursue prospective talent through networking, or lend support to executives other than those they report to. They also ask questions. Most Hollywood executives like to talk about themselves, so it's smart to pose questions in terms of their experience. For example, don't ask, "What are the responsibilities of a development executive?" Instead ask, "When you were developing *Titanic*, what were your primary responsibilities?"

SAMPLE PROJECT

It's widely known in the industry that your record label is looking to sign new talent. You're constantly fielding calls from the managers of the "next big band," and you have to determine which are worth your executive's time. Your phone rings late Friday, and you listen to a manager describe a hot new client that is performing this weekend. Though you know your boss will not want to talk to the manager, you ask for the time and location. You go to hear the band and decide that your boss may want to consider this prospect. On Monday you look for a rare free moment when you can tell her about the band. After much persuading, you convince her to talk to the band's manager. Provided the conversation goes well, you'll earn points with your boss and the company. If it doesn't, be prepared for a tongue-lashing.

A DAY IN THE LIFE OF AN EXECUTIVE ASSISTANT

7:00   Get up, shower, dress, and make yourself a quick bite to eat.

8:00   Take the subway to work.

8:45   Walk from the subway station to your office against a chill wind. Consider giving up the late-night excitement of New York for the sunshine of Los Angeles.

9:00   Check voice mail and e-mails and schedule calls for your boss to return. Go to the kitchen to make a pot of coffee and grab a jelly doughnut.

9:15   Read the trade papers, *Billboard* and *R&R*.

9:30   By now the rest of the office has arrived, and the phone is ringing incessantly. Forward only the most important calls and assure the other callers that your boss will get back to them as soon as possible.

10:30   Mention to your boss that you saw a hot new band last night that has yet to sign with a major label.

10:45   Make reservations for your boss and associates at a top restaurant. Call the associates to confirm the meeting time and place.

11:00   Discuss the state of the industry with fellow executive assistants. Gossip about who's coming and going in the office.

12:00   Go to lunch with coworkers. Expense it, of course.

1:00   Get blasted by your boss for no reason other than that you're the only one who will tolerate it.

1:30   Send a mass fax to your company's Los Angeles and Nashville offices.

2:15   Field a call from the executive's husband. Promise to remind your boss of their dinner plans tonight.

2:45   Set up a conference call and listen as your boss and executives from the parent company discuss the music division's performance for the past quarter.

4:00   Finish reading the trades.

4:30   Compose and send a memo from your boss to the entire division explaining that, in an effort to rein in excessive spending, there will be no more free lunches.

5:30   Remind your boss of her dinner plans tonight.

6:00   Leave the office.

7:00   Meet some friends for dinner at a cheap Chinese restaurant, then catch a hot new band that's playing in the East Village.

10:30   Realize the band isn't so hot. Leave the bar and head home.

Development Executive

Before a movie hits the big screen, it goes through a long development process. During this preproduction period, development executives work with writers to turn ideas into scripts or shape an existing script into a suitable final draft.

As is true in other executive positions, there's no small amount of stress in these jobs. If a movie doesn't do well at the box office, in video sales, or in foreign markets, it could affect the performance of the entire entertainment conglomerate—and as a result, there's pressure to choose potential hits and develop them to their full market potential.

Development executives also have to deal with the frustration of having projects put on the shelf. Even when a production company spends millions of dollars to purchase and rewrite a script, it may later decide to discontinue the project if its financial potential does not look good. Development executives usually have experience as assistants to development executives, and sometimes as story editors. Their backgrounds are varied, but all development executives must like to read and write, as they are constantly providing coverage of scripts. Development departments exist at both film production companies and movie studios.

THE WORK

As an insider says, "Development is all about writers." If you're not developing an existing project with one writer, you're listening to a pitch from another. And executives must have writing skills themselves to provide coverage of film scripts. Unlike marketing or distribution executives, development executives may be involved in a movie from inception to completion, sometimes earning an associate producer or producer credit. "It is impossible for me to say that any one personality will excel more than others," an insider says. "However, in general, if you're going to work in development, you need to have a love for movies; you need to be a good writer and enjoy reading; and you must be sociable because a lot of it is soliciting new material through networking."

SAMPLE PROJECT

After reading a spec script from a relatively unknown writer, you grant him a meeting. The plot was average, but the character development and dialogue were some of the best you've read. The script is not your type of project, but you would like to hear some of the writer's other story ideas. In the meeting, he pitches a teen comedy about a serial killer. With the right talent, it might be relatively inexpensive to produce. Still, the subject matter is touchy—it could kill or be killed at the box office. You have to decide whether to pitch this to someone who can green-light it.

> **If you're going to work in development, you need to have a love for movies, you need to be a good writer and enjoy reading, and you must be sociable because a lot of it is soliciting new material through networking.**

A DAY IN THE LIFE OF A DEVELOPMENT EXECUTIVE

7:00   Jump out of bed and into the shower.

8:45   Arrive at the office. Skim *Daily Variety*, *The Hollywood Reporter*, and the *Los Angeles Times*.

10:00   Make calls to three agents who've sent you film scripts. Explain that you're not interested in a period piece, a musical, or a weepy drama.

11:00   Listen to a 23-year-old writer (the son of one of the studio head's friends) explain why his sci-fi romantic comedy would revolutionize the film industry.

12:00   Contact the agents of possible writers for your current project in development, a thriller.

12:45   Drive to a Beverly Hills restaurant for lunch with a writer you want to have rewrite another project.

2:00 Speed-read a spec script a name agent is pushing really hard. Not bad, but not for you.

3:00 Meet with a writer to discuss another project you have in development, a romantic comedy. Explain to the writer that you want to develop the subplot and secondary characters.

5:00 Make more calls to agents to pass on scripts.

7:00 Attend a Hollywood gala commemorating the progress of African Americans in film. Network, network, network.

9:00 Read another script at home. Teen comedies are the trend these days, so you have to wade through 120 pages of high-school angst.

Publicity Coordinator

So the television program, movie, or CD has been developed and produced. Now what? It's time to sell the entertainment product, that's what. This is where the publicity department plays a role. Its primary job is to make the artists in an entertainment product—and the entertainment product itself—more visible in the marketplace. Publicity does this by working with various media outlets—television, radio, and newspapers and magazines—to get the company's product covered on the air or in print. One big task of the publicity department is to set up interviews with the performing artists the entertainment company has under contract. Those interviews with actors starring in just-released movies or hit television shows on *The Tonight Show* or *Entertainment Tonight*? They're the result of publicists' work. And those reviews of new CDs in *People* and *Details*, or that article about an upcoming concert tour in *Rolling Stone*? Yup—those are, too.

THE WORK

People in publicity are responsible for all of the details of getting the artists in the public eye. This includes overseeing the production of a press kit—a collection of information—artist bios, photos, product descriptions, and CDs or film clips—for each artist or new CD, movie, or television show. Publicity people also set up press junkets or artist interviews and photo shoots with various media outlets.

The work requires a strong attention to detail. You've got to make sure the artist understands when the interview is and what message he or she should give about the product; you've got to make sure the press kit is assembled and sent to the magazines before their next-issue deadlines. If you're not good with maintaining schedules or meeting deadlines, publicity is not the place for you.

You also have to be comfortable dealing with a lot of people with a lot of different needs and points of view. You interact with everyone from the artists, to their managers, to members of the press, to coworkers in other departments of your company— and you've got to get along with all of them, at least if you want to do well in your job and move ahead. One upside of this is that you end up with a large and varied group of contacts—and sometimes even friends—who can help you as you move forward in your entertainment career.

You've also got to be proactive, creative, and have a go-getter attitude. The media are overloaded with entertainment publicity pieces; if you can make your company's publicity stand out from everything else out there, you have a good chance of increasing its revenues—and getting yourself promoted.

SAMPLE PROJECT

One of your artists, who lives in Montana, is scheduled for an appearance two weeks from Tuesday on *Late Night with David Letterman*. A British journalist at a big magazine wants to do a face-to-face interview and photo shoot with the artist, and you set something up in New York City for the same day the artist is appearing on Letterman. Then you learn that, because of a scheduling conflict, the Letterman date must change from Tuesday to Friday. As a result, the artist will not be in New York on the scheduled date. You call your U.K. press office to contact the journalist to make sure she gets the schedule change and adjusts her plans accordingly.

A DAY IN THE LIFE OF A PUBLICIST

8:30   Get to work. Check e-mails and voice mail. Return call from a journalist in Chicago who wants to set up a face-to-face interview with one of the bands on your label when its tour passes through town next month. Return another call from one of the marketing people in your company, concerning the publicity strategy for one of your label's upcoming CD releases.

9:30   Set up interviews between Belgian and French journalists and two of your artists whose CDs are about to release in Europe.

11:00   One of your rock artists is going to tour Portugal and Finland in a couple of months, so you call your company's label managers in those countries to make sure that they're ready to support the artist—by attending the artist's shows and taking advantage of local publicity opportunities. Learn that the artist's new CD hasn't yet been released in Finland; discuss with the label manager in Finland how it would be excellent to release it now, before the Finland concert.

12:30   Head out to lunch.

1:30   Back from lunch. Check e-mails and voice mail. Call label managers in Japan and Australia to discuss upcoming tours by a couple of your label's artists in those countries.

2:30   E-mail the manager of one of your label's artists to let her know about upcoming deadlines on press kit requests. A couple of magazines need the artist's press kit, which is missing the artwork because the artist hasn't approved it yet, by Thursday. And a foreign newspaper needs the press kit by Friday.

3:00 Call the manager of another artist. Several journalists want to do 20-minute "phoners"—phone interviews—with the artist next week, and the manager needs to contact the artist to schedule times for the calls.

4:00 Time for the Wednesday marketing meeting. Wednesday morning is when SoundScan—the Billboard Top 200—is released, and you discuss it in addition to your artists' press exposure and sales trends.

5:30 Call a journalist to confirm a short interview-and-photo-shoot session before one of your band's shows tonight.

6:00 Head home. Once home, go for a short run, then take a shower and eat some dinner.

9:00 Oversee the interview and photo shoot before the band's show at the Whiskey. Cut it short when it's clear the journalist isn't about to stop asking questions even though the band has to get ready to go onstage.

11:30 The show's over, so you head home. The band is red-hot live, which is good to know, so you can talk knowledgeably about it in your work. Pop the band's CD in on the drive home to get better acquainted with it.

The Big Picture: Sports

Here's a sampling of positions in different departments and areas of the sports biz.

As far as working in the leagues goes, there's a clear hierarchy in terms of pay and prestige: Popular sports are above less-popular sports, major leagues are above minor leagues, and strong teams are above weaker ones. How much you make is a function of where your organization fits into these rankings. The great thing about working for the minors—aside from the fact that they are easier to get into—is that you'll get more exposure to different jobs. This will not only allow you to refine your career goals early on, but will also give you a leg up on your competition when you decide you want to move up to the majors.

MARKETING

VP of Marketing

Oversees all efforts to support sponsorship and ticket-sales staff with marketing, advertising, and campaigns.

Salary range: $60,000 to $150,000 or more

Director of Promotions

Creates innovative or popular promotions, including giveaways, contests, and concerts, to increase attendance.

Salary range: $30,000 to $70,000

Director of Community Relations

Partners with charities and other nonprofit organizations to help players and the team bond with the community.

Salary range: $30,000 to $70,000

Manager of Community Relations

Oversees one or more ongoing projects; supports the director.

Salary range: $30,000 to $40,000

Marketing Coordinator

Creates brochures and other marketing materials; supports supervisor; makes lots of copies.

Salary range: $20,000 to $40,000

Sports Marketing Manager

Works as part of a corporation's larger marketing team; finds marketing opportunities with leagues, teams, and events that fit in with the larger marketing strategy to make sure brand managers' needs are met; negotiates with properties owners; oversees ad agency relationship.

Salary range: $50,000 to $100,000

SALES

Account Executive, Ticket Sales

Sells group and season tickets to companies, organizations, and individuals.

Salary range: $20,000 to $40,000

SPONSORSHIPS

Senior Director/VP of Sponsorships

Sells sponsorships to companies; oversees three to five directors.

Salary range: $100,000 to $125,000

Director of Sponsorships

Does some selling of sponsorships to companies; manages one to three accounts to make sure they are happy and that they renew or sign up for additional sponsorship deals; oversees account managers.

Salary range: $75,000 to $85,000

Account Manager

Works with client team to execute sponsorship plans.

Salary range: $50,000 to $70,000

PUBLICITY/MEDIA RELATIONS

Information Director

Compiles and distributes all statistics; handles player interview requests.

Salary range: $40,000 to $55,000

Media Services Manager

Ensures all members of the press are properly credentialed and have parking passes.

Salary range: $40,000 to $55,000

Media Relations Assistant

Compiles game notes; distributes information to the press; puts together the media guide.

Salary range: $25,000 to $38,000

PROGRAMMING DEPARTMENT

Director of Programming

On behalf of all of the leagues' teams, negotiates network and cable television distribution deals for games and nongame programming.

Salary range: $75,000 to $85,000

LEGAL DEPARTMENT

General Counsel

Advises league management on all aspects of labor law, sponsorship and licensing contracts, liability, and litigation.

Salary range: $50,000 to $120,000

SPORTS AGENCY

Agent

Recruits athletes as clients; negotiates player contracts; evaluates and negotiates endorsement and appearance deals; manages client's finances.

Salary range: $40,000 to millions of dollars

Athlete Relations Coordinator

Handles scheduling for clients; coordinates events; screens incoming offers; maintains press book on clients.

Salary range: $25,000 to $45,000

Director of Sponsorships

Corporate sponsorships have become a lucrative revenue stream for teams and leagues. Essentially, what you're selling is advertising—signage, really. Sponsorships go a bit deeper, though. Instead of just buying airtime or a billboard, sponsors buy *into* the event or property itself, becoming a part of it. This is evident when every flat surface is covered with the sponsor's logo, and it's even more obvious when the sponsor's name is grafted onto the name of the event or facility.

People who work in sponsorship sales at the league level need not only basic sales skills, but pretty advanced business knowledge. Their clients are brand managers and high-level marketers, so they have to be able to show them benefits that will be meaningful to them on their terms. In fact, many sponsorship people at the league level have MBAs. Those who don't have gained a lot of on-the-job-experience in the sports industry or elsewhere.

Sponsorships is an excellent area to pursue if you are business minded and aggressive. However, if you lack these attributes, close proximity to your better-paid clients may induce you to seek work in advertising or consumer goods. The money's better, and you can still maintain a connection with sports.

THE WORK

At the director level, about 25 percent of your time is spent on sales. This includes doing research to identify likely prospects, cold calling, and setting up meetings, presentations, and client-schmoozing sessions, usually focused on games. The other 75 percent is taken up with managing your current accounts. You have to be comfortable in creatively structuring deals that will appeal to your client, but you also have to oversee the execution. And that definitely means sweating the small stuff and dealing with a lot of people inside and outside of your company, in addition to the client. You also have to be an advocate for your league and its teams, making sure that its image is upheld and its logos are used properly on other properties.

SAMPLE PROJECT

You're in charge of sponsorships for the Slam Dunk contest, and Gatorade is the main sponsor. Make sure the commercials are trafficked on the networks properly, and during the broadcast, make sure the TV billboards advertising the sponsor look good. Make sure all on-court signs are correct. You also have to take care of the key client executives: make sure that there are enough tickets for them and that they are in the right place in the stadium, arena, or wherever the event takes place. Once the execs are inside, take them to the court and ensure that the athletes are doing face-time with them. Gatorade is giving out samples, so you also have to make sure that sample locations are in the right places and that product is actually making it into the hands of attendees.

A DAY IN THE LIFE OF A DIRECTOR OF SPONSORSHIPS

6:30   Wake up.

7:00   Hit the gym near your house.

8:30   Arrive at the office and clear through e-mails that have come in.

9:00	Attend the daily NBA All-Star update meeting. One week to go, so everyone director level and higher is very careful to log his or her progress, discuss any snags, and work out resolutions. No surprises, people.
10:00	Meet with your team, give them a rundown of the meeting, and discuss their to-dos for the week.
10:30	Start calling clients and internal departments. The folks from Coke have faxed over their VIP list. Make sure that it's passed on to the right people so that they have tickets and a couple of players to talk to before the game. Confirm that Gatorade has talent lined up for the game. Call your boss to let him know.
12:00	Eat lunch at your desk.
12:30	Look at last-minute materials. Mentally walk through the schedule of events.
1:30	Think of other programs to pitch to current clients, like a new 4-year presentation package.
3:00	Spend the rest of the afternoon on a critical PowerPoint presentation; get internal approval.
6:00	Meet a new prospective client at a Knicks game.
9:30	Have a quick drink with the prospective client and then head home.

Media Relations Assistant

Media interest in most pro teams is so strong that a dedicated media relations staff is essential to satisfying as many demands as possible while at the same time making sure that the team is getting the best news coverage it can possibly get. While the marketing team is out supporting the sales team, the PR team has the press as its main client. Media relations is an excellent way to start out in sports. The positions are fairly plentiful, you can quickly get up to speed on the mechanics of how a team works, and the culture is pretty relaxed, since your job duties are not directly tied to revenue. The downside to this last point is that media relations can equate to something of a holding pen for a bunch of not particularly ambitious people. They get on well with the sales and marketing folks, but insiders say that there is a clear if unspoken division between the two camps. Still, for people who want lots of access to players and close proximity to the game, media relations is an excellent option.

THE WORK

One of the main jobs of a media relations assistant is to act as a liaison between the players and the media. This means helping journalists get interviews and photo shoots with players and prepping the players so they know to whom they are speaking and what the questions will be about. They also must make sure that the press has every conceivable piece of background information possible at their fingertips, and they must accurately enter each game's statistics into a database maintained by the league.

Media relations staff work closely with athletes. "They see us more than they see their family," says one insider. That may be, but athletes are like clients to the media relations people, who must maintain professionalism at all times. (Postgame socialization is permitted to varying degrees depending on the team. It's often discouraged, though.) In this role, the ability to deal with a variety of people and serve their needs efficiently and cheerfully is crucial. Flexibility is also key, since you'll often have to cover for people both inside and outside of your department. A college degree, usually in journalism, English, or a sports-related major, is required.

SAMPLE PROJECT

A key duty for PR people is getting the press box ready on game day. This means everything from compiling the day's game notes (including information on your team and the opposing team) to making copies and distributing them to drawing up a seating chart for the press. During and after the game, you have to be available to journalists, who may have a question about something that just happened on the field or who might request some historical statistic that will have to be researched quickly so that they can make their deadlines.

A DAY IN THE LIFE OF A MEDIA RELATIONS ASSISTANT

7:30   Wake up and eat breakfast.

9:00   Get to work, make some coffee, and download stats from the league. Update your team's stats and those on league leaders, and also pull stats for the opposing team. Print copies of everything and get them ready to be distributed to team management and the press.

9:30   Go to various news websites and pull clips covering the previous day's game. Photocopy everything relating to your team and the opposing team, as well as any other league news of note. Print this out so that team management will know what's going on in the league and so that the writers covering your team will know what other writers are writing about.

10:30   The visiting team's PR staff has just sent in updated notes. Throw the old ones in the recycling bin and start copying and collating again.

11:00   Set up the press box. Put all of the info on a back table for the writers to browse through. Some writers like their info already placed at their seats, so make sure they are taken care of. Post a new seating chart, making sure everyone has an assigned seat.

11:30   Pull together minor-league stats and clippings for the coaching staff. Hand out the same material to the opposing team. Continually run off copies of new lineups, notes, and other info for the press as it comes in.

12:00   Grab lunch from Subway and eat at desk while checking e-mail from the past few hours.

12:45   More copying.

2:30   Players arrive. Help facilitate interviews and video shoots for a couple of hours.

4:30   A cancer society arrives to do a scheduled meet-and-greet. Go get them from the stands and escort them down to the field. Introduce them to the players and take a few pictures of them with the players, using their cameras. Bring them back up to the stands.

5:00   Eat catered dinner with the rest of the staff. Keep hoping for Indian food, just once, but no, it's pizza again.

6:00   Meet the press as they come in, and chat with them about the game. Handle any last-minute requests.

7:00   Game starts. You're scheduled to do play-by-play for the entire game. At the same time, with one eye on the field, write up the post-game notes for a post-game release your boss will put together.

10:00   Print up the notes and give them to media members.

10:30   Lock up the press box. Go back to office and enter all of the game stats into the league database.

11:00   Go home.

Athlete Coordinator

The agent is always out finding new clients and doing deals for the existing clients. He's also taking care of whatever legal issues may arise on a daily basis. To make sure he's freed up to bring in the big bucks, he needs someone to filter requests, deal with minor athlete issues, and generally keep the athletes happy. That's where the athlete coordinator comes in. This person takes away all of the worrying about how to make appearances fit into athletes' schedules and makes sure things proceed as smoothly as possible. In order to do well in this position, you must be very organized and energetic. Keeping track of up to 35 athletes' daily schedules can get quite hectic. You must also be able to communicate with others and take the initiative to find the answers you need.

THE WORK

Much of what athlete coordinators do is on the spur of the moment and has to happen *now*. They make sure that the sponsors are following through on their end of the contract and that the athletes stay true to their end, too. They screen and prioritize requests for demos, interviews, and appearances. They will even negotiate prices for athlete appearances, using guidelines established by the agent. Then, of course, they might go to the event to make sure everything goes smoothly. Coordinators clip magazine articles featuring their athletes to create a press book, which the PR department uses to pitch stories. They schedule athletes' calendars, including events, demos, team trips, and photo shoots. The athletes come to them to see what they are doing for the week. And it doesn't stop at just booking an athlete's schedule. They may ask the coordinator to book travel for them along with ten friends. This is a high-stress position because you are never off the clock. If the athlete is stuck at the airport at midnight and no one is there to pick him up, it's the coordinator who will have to deal with it. That's why coordinators have to be extremely organized as well as advance planners, working to prevent snags from happening as much as possible.

SAMPLE PROJECT

You follow through on interview requests every day. Most often it's just setting up a time when the athlete and interviewer can get together on the phone. But other times you get a list of questions e-mailed to you and you have to stay on the athletes to answer them by the interviewer's deadline. This includes a daily follow-up call: "How are you doing with those questions? Did you get a hold of 'press' today?"

A DAY IN THE LIFE OF AN ATHLETE COORDINATOR

7:00   Jump out of bed and into the shower.

8:00   Arrive at the office. Check e-mail and voice mail.

9:00   Add various requests from your messages to the to-do list you created last night.

10:00   Start working on to-do list.

10:10   Interrupted throughout the day. Field call after call for athlete appearance requests and approvals for sponsors.

12:45   Give an athlete a ride to the airport. He's not even on his way to a personal appearance. He's off on a Hawaiian vacation for the second time this year. You've never even been to Hawaii!

1:45   Grab drive-through grub on your way back to the office.

2:00   Back in the office, there are three athlete requests waiting for you. One is a guy who wants to cancel a photo shoot for a sports magazine. You have to explain to the editor that he *will* do it eventually. The other two are requests for you to book travel plans.

3:00   Process several invoices for athlete winning incentives and victory incentives.

5:00   Out the door, but the day isn't over!

5:30   Arrive home and get back on wireless Internet/e-mail.

6:00   Continue to receive incoming athlete appearance requests and requests from the athletes themselves.

7:00   Write up a to-do list for tomorrow. Did you get anything off your to-do list for today? Maybe one or two items . . .

The Workplace

Lifestyle

Culture

Workplace Diversity

Hours

Travel

Compensation

Career Notes

Insider Scoop

Lifestyle

While some jobs are just a way to pay the bills, others are a person's life. Working in sports or entertainment generally determines not only your hours and compensation, but also your leisure activities and social network. Your way of life varies according to the position, but a few characteristics are common throughout the industry: The work is intense, the hours long, and your job encompasses more than just your workday. "One misconception about entertainment and sports is that people don't work hard," says an insider. "The business moves in a split second. The volume of work can be staggering."

People who work in film, television, or music are passionate about their medium, and people in sports are passionate about their sport and team. All employees have to stay on top of developing trends—a task that can be accomplished only through total immersion. The business is the constant topic of conversation. Of course, monitoring the state of film, television, music, or sports may be more appealing than selling insurance, but it has its price. "It's not very stimulating because all people talk about is entertainment or sports," one insider says. Another says, "If you can do something else, do it. If you can't, then you're suited for the industry."

Networking is a big part of the entertainment business. To do well, you've got to spend time at industry-related events like premieres, concerts, and awards ceremonies, as well as at less formal gatherings like parties and lunch get-togethers. There's no doubt about it: This is a relationship business. When you're at the start of your career, networking helps you get promotions or find new jobs. And later, when you're in a role with more decision-making power, networking will allow you to explore all of your options in terms of getting deals done and projects moving forward. "Perception is reality," says an insider. "If you're not visible, you're not really there."

Sports is also a relationship business, where deals are made and jobs found via the people you know. But it tends to be more cyclical in that it follows the playing season of whatever sport you're involved with. When your sport is in season, you may end up practically living at the stadium. The lifestyle of sports is a bit less manic than that of the entertainment business. One insider who started at a film studio and then switched to working for a pro team says, "In entertainment, a lot of your success is oriented around who you know. The doors are a little harder to open. In sports, you can find your way in easier, because more than anything else, it's hard work that will get you noticed."

> **One misconception about entertainment and sports is that people don't work hard. The business moves in a split second. The volume of work can be staggering.**

Culture

In the past few decades, film, television, and music have increasingly focused on youthful audiences, and in the process the workplace has grown younger, too. While there are more than a few wily veterans in the entertainment game, expect to be surrounded mainly by other young people—nearly all of them in love with their chosen medium.

The youthfulness of the industry has helped create other aspects of its culture. Along with the focus on creative products, there's an informality that encourages individuality and self-expression. "I can wear jeans to work every day," says an insider. "In fact, I could wear sweatpants if I wanted to. And the people I work with are a very eclectic group." This is a hip industry: If you work here, there's a good chance you'll spend your free time shopping for the right clothes and the right car, and spending getaway weekends in hot vacation spots. It's also an industry that knows it's hip; you'll hear more than a few disparaging jokes about Midwesterners as you work out at the gym or order your sushi dinner.

While entertainment companies generally have liberal work environments compared with the rest of corporate America—employees don't often have to dress like bankers or keep a tight rein on their personality quirks—business practices and cultures vary greatly among the industry players. According to one insider, "Paramount maintains most of the Hollywood traditions and is very conservative, whereas Universal is more progressive." Of course, "conservative" and "progressive" are subjective terms. An entertainment company might be called conservative, for example, if it stresses professionalism and maintains a somewhat formal workplace hierarchy; another company might be called progressive because it offers perks such as domestic partner benefits.

Job seekers should research the backgrounds and attitudes of the top executives, as they tend to determine a company's culture. Walt Disney Company CEO and chairman Michael Eisner says, "I go for talent and put up with a lot of peculiar behavior, none of which I judge as long as people are basically ethical and moral," and it's no coincidence that industry insiders describe Disney as very liberal. Talk to as many contacts as possible, both within the companies you're interested in and elsewhere in the industry; you'll learn a lot about companies' cultures that way.

The industry has always had an entrepreneurial culture, so you won't find much structure. As an insider says, "It's hard work, and nothing's going to be given to you. You have to be disciplined." All you have to do to vault to the top is have one major success—produce one blockbuster movie, find one platinum-selling musical artist, or develop one hit television series. This is great, unless you're not producing successes for your company. In that case, you either languish in your low-level position until the people around you all but ignore you, or you're forced to find work in another industry—a depressing prospect, given the way people in other industries often don't respect the skills learned in entertainment. All this adds up to a lot of pressure; those who do succeed develop thick skins along the way. "You learn to watch your fellow workers fail," says an insider.

The pressure to succeed leads to a lot of cutthroat competition. True stories abound about entertainment executives screwing people they call friends just to get ahead. The pressure, along with the way the industry pushes very young people into very senior positions—often when they're just a few years out of college—also leads to a lot of swollen egos and displays of immaturity. One insider says, "Executives often confuse themselves with the talent." Another says, "The emotional abuse is difficult, but it's part of the job."

Finally, because of the vagaries of the entertainment industry's culture, there's a lot of cynicism among people working in it. An insider speaks for many when she says, "I'm fascinated by this business. I love it, and I hate it."

"Love-hate" is not a term that applies to sports careers. Insiders typically speak of their passion for their sport: "I love going to the ball park every day. I grew up playing sports, and I loved baseball the most, though ironically it was the sport I was the worst at. I love that my career is oriented around athletics."

An insider who has worked in both entertainment and sports says, "The people and atmosphere are completely different. It almost seems that people in entertainment are on edge all of the time. Sports people are more relaxed, almost like a family." Sports people are also in much closer proximity to their audiences than entertainment people are. They see firsthand the excitement fans feel at a game, and they strive to provide an environment that is family friendly and always entertaining. Sports is a customer-service driven industry, in sharp contrast to the entertainment business. That means that most people in the business are generally nicer.

Dennis Rodman aside, the culture of the sports industry is more conservative than in the entertainment industry where creative types run amok. Insiders say that geographic location has something to do with it. Sports jobs are distributed throughout the country, not isolated in New York (with the exception of the major governing bodies) or L.A., so sports-industry folks working in, say, Minneapolis tend to dress and act like other professionals living in that city. At its most formal, dress code in the sports biz is business casual—khakis and polo shirts. On stressful game days, when comfort is paramount, shorts and T-shirts are the norm, though team employees often wear matching polo shirts during the game itself, so that they can be identified as staff.

Also, many of the best sports jobs—whether they involve sales, marketing, or sports management—involve face-time with corporate types from other industries. An ad salesperson working for a team may have a dream job from an advertiser's perspective, but he or she still needs to wear a suit to meetings.

Workplace Diversity

While there are some very powerful female executives in Hollywood, the upper echelons of the business side of entertainment are overwhelmingly white and male. However, as the industry becomes increasingly younger, it's also becoming more diverse. An insider says the industry is looking for "well-rounded individuals with different, eclectic backgrounds."

The sports segment is, as you'd expect, even more white and male. There are high-profile women in marketing, management, and other functions, but the ratio is nowhere near 50:50. And other minorities are hardly better served. Gene Upshaw, chairman of the NFL Players Association, once mentioned how common it was for him to be the only black person in the room during contract negotiations.

See the "Additional Resources" section of this guide to learn more about opportunities for women and ethnic minorities in entertainment.

Hours

Younger members of the film, movie, and television business work about 50-hour weeks. As you move up the ranks, your working hours grow along with your responsibility and involvement. And more and more of your working hours are spent outside the office. For example, an executive at a film studio, television network, or record label may spend as few as 10 hours a week in the office, but log long hours networking with industry executives or sampling prospective film, television, or music properties. The higher you climb, the more you need to think of your entertainment position as a way of life rather than just a job.

In sports, the hours are usually nine to five during the off-season. During the season, however, 13- or 14-hour days are not uncommon, especially on game days. Marketers and salespeople in the leagues work at least 50 hours per week year-round. Sports managers work 50 to 60 hours a week or more, though some of that might be after they get home. In fact, agents are often available around the clock for their clients.

Travel

The amount of travel varies depending on your position—if you're a record-label A&R executive scouting talent, you travel some; if you work in film production, you may spend months at a time on location in some out-of-the-way place. But in general there's not much travel in entertainment, unless you consider driving from Hollywood to Burbank an extended trip. This is primarily because Los Angeles and New York are the hubs of the film, television, and music businesses, so there's little need to venture beyond their boundaries.

Travel in sports also varies widely. If you're in a team's front office, you won't have much reason to travel, unless you work in publicity, in which case you follow the team wherever it goes. If you're an agent or marketer, you'll often travel to meet athletes and sponsors or oversee advertising spots and the execution of events. As a general rule, the higher up you are, insiders say, the more you will travel.

Compensation

The high demand for entry-level positions allows sports and entertainment companies to keep wages for the people who fill them low. In the case of sports, at least, one insider offers this explanation: "Leagues are not like normal companies. They are associations owned by the team owners. The money that goes to employee salaries comes out of their pockets. It's like working for a family business in that respect." An entertainment insider has this to say: "At the lower rungs, you don't have a lot of bargaining power. You can be replaced really cheaply, because everybody and his brother wants in to the industry." Recent college graduates can expect a yearly salary in the $20,000s. Likewise, law school graduates and MBAs do not command as much money as they do in other industries. A lawyer with no sports entertainment experience, for example, will be paid in the low $40,000s to high $50,000s.

If you survive your term as a grunt, though, you'll find that high-ranking executives are compensated about as well as those in most other industries. For instance, a vice president of publicity with a number of years of experience can expect a salary in the $100,000 range, as can similarly qualified executives in other departments. An insider says, "The higher you go, the more money you make, and the less you have to pay for—you can negotiate all kinds of things into your contract, like car insurance and laptops that you get to keep if you leave the company." The one area where it's possible to make a fortune is in sports management, but you have to remember that for every agent making tens of millions off of Tiger Woods' hundreds of millions, there are countless others struggling to get by.

VACATION

The entertainment industry works hard, but it plays hard, too. Entertainment companies tend to be generous with vacation time. The more structured conglomerates may offer the standard two to three weeks of vacation, but smaller production companies are likely to give considerably more. Smaller companies and even some bigger ones typically close down from the middle of December until just after the New Year. The industry also celebrates holidays not typically recognized by other industries; no one in film, television, or music works the day after the Oscar, Emmy, or Grammy awards shows, respectively. In sports, you'll find vacation time during off-season fairly generous, to offset the low pay and also as an admission that there just isn't as much work to be done then. Vacations are a no-no during the season, however.

PERKS

Perks for entry-level personnel include free merchandise (CDs; sports, movie or television-show baseball caps and jackets; leftover wardrobe items from movie or television productions; etc.); tickets to movie screenings, concerts, and sports events; occasional free meals; promotional items; and sometimes a chance to meet celebrities and star athletes. As your level of responsibility grows, so do your perks.

Career Notes

It's important to understand that careers in entertainment do not follow a predetermined sequence of job roles. Entry-level hires usually begin in support positions and spend several years there. After that, whether and when they get promoted to an executive position is contingent on the company, the opportunities, and the individual.

As well, with the trend toward vertical integration, people can move laterally from one division to another—an assistant in film distribution may pursue a job in television distribution if it appears to have better career-boosting potential, for example. But most people stick with one segment of the industry. "Focusing on one thing in this business is important," says an insider. "Players differ in each area of the business. You need to know the specific community and how people work."

People generally decide whether to remain in the industry within their first few years. As one insider puts it, "The industry loses a lot of people because they don't want to put up with the bullshit." Those who stay do so for two reasons. First, they're passionate about their work. "There is something special about being able to work in an industry where you care about the product," says an insider. Second, the transition from entertainment to another industry isn't easy. According to an insider, "Other industries don't take entertainment seriously. It's branded as all glamour, but it's much more than that."

There's also the potential for being labeled a "sports guy." For people who intend to stay in the business, that's fine. But advancement is slow in sports, and the pay is low; people who want to move to another industry, especially in a business capacity, may find their work experience is not viewed as seriously as it should be.

For those trying to break into sports, however, being branded "a sports guy (or gal)" is exactly what you want. Competition for the lowest slots is intense, so it's important to

>> **There is something special about being able to work in an industry where you care about the product.**

give the impression you know your way around your preferred sport. Most people start as interns or volunteers and find opportunities once they've made it inside. Less frequently, some job seekers find out about openings from friends and use their contacts to score an interview. This will help, but knowledge of sports and some relevant work experience are still pretty important.

Once people land their first job, they find that they tend to advance slowly. Many people stay in the same jobs for years or even decades. To advance your career, flexibility is key. If you're a PR person with a lifer above you, you will need to either develop new skills and move to another department or take your PR skills to a new organization, perhaps in another part of the country, if you want to move up and earn more.

The one skill that is universally respected in sports is the ability to bring money into your organization. If you can prove to the powers-that-be that your promotions have increased ticket sales or that your merchandising idea was a cost-effective hit, for example, they will be eager to give you more responsibility—and money. One insider says, "You aren't going to get paid extremely well unless you can prove you are worth it. There are a million people out there who want your job and will do it for less."

Insider Scoop

WHAT PEOPLE REALLY LIKE

Glamour

Everybody wants to be entertained, and four of the most popular forms of entertainment are television, film, music, and sports. It can be a real rush to walk into a theater or turn on the television or radio and say, "I helped make that."

Room to Grow

Making a film, television show, or recording all involve writing, performing, and producing. While you can build a career in any one of those areas, success in one area can lead to an opportunity and even a career in another. And as one industry insider tells us, "The hyphenate [writer-director] is the real king of Hollywood." In sports, selling is king. If you can match that with your other skills, you can almost write your own ticket.

Relaxed Atmosphere

The entertainment industry is an energetic, creative field. Office decor and workplace dress are often more like what you'd see at a nightclub than at a typical office. And if you move up the chain of command, don't be surprised if your office is an exclusive bar or restaurant—that's where many deals are made. Things rarely get so elegant in the sports world, but the atmosphere is usually relaxed—familial, even.

Creativity

"Entertainment executives are looking for two different things in a prospective project," one insider says. "The first is something that has proven commercial in the past. The second is just the opposite, something that surprises you, something that might just stand out in the marketplace." If you want to redefine the way people think about society and culture, this might be the field for you.

WATCH OUT!

Low Starting Pay

Everyone in sports and entertainment—except the very well connected—starts at the bottom. In one of the most common entry-level entertainment positions, production assistant (a glorified gofer), you sort mail, make copies, even pick up dry cleaning. The hours are long and hard, the pay poor. The trade-offs: You get to play a role in projects that will be seen by millions of people, you get to do a lot of networking, and if you're smart, diligent, and lucky, you eventually move into a high-paying executive position.

Superficiality

Not everyone in Hollywood is pretentious and superficial, but many people in the industry are. And outside the film and television world, you may be viewed as just another out-of-touch Hollywood snob. Sure, some will revere you for working in a creative, dynamic field, but others will look at you with a mocking eye. And when you work on the business side, you certainly encounter ignorance from people outside entertainment. "The rest of America has no idea what we do," one insider says.

Egos

While some executives are fast-talking, morally compromised deal-makers, others are soul-searching creators. No matter which type you work for, keep in mind that they often have little or no regard for the new kid on the block. Prepare yourself for a tongue lashing if you deliver the great one's coffee with two sugars instead of three. "There are some real jerks in this business," says an insider. Sports is less rough and tumble, but there is a clear hierarchy in any organization, and you would do well to respect it.

Lack of Transferable Experience

Sports and entertainment jobs are often not good preparation for jobs in other fields. Even if you work in a position that's common to many large companies, such as marketing or publicity, people in other industries may not take your experience seriously.

The Money-Go-Round

Entertainment and sports companies are filled with fans who love the media or sport they work in. Money has always been a part of the equation, but the influx of corporate America onto the playing field, the screen, and the stage can be disheartening. Especially when the big guys are making the bread, and all you're getting are the crumbs.

Getting Hired

The Recruiting Process

Interviewing Tips

Getting Grilled

Grilling Your Interviewer

The Final Word

The Recruiting Process

As entertainment companies consolidate, they're developing more extensive human resources departments. They're also using new technologies such as the Internet to recruit candidates. But traditionally, entertainment companies do not rely on human resources to staff their companies; rather, they bank on their reputations and the allure of the industry to attract prospective employees—not to mention nepotism, which remains common. In other words, companies in this industry don't do much recruiting. In candidates' struggles to get noticed and in the door, the key is having the right contacts. "It's not what you know or even whom you know, but who knows you," says one insider. The same holds true for sports companies, though their recruiting efforts are even less advanced. Scour the websites of your favorite teams or league, as jobs listings may be posted there and nowhere else.

Here are several tips from insiders:

- Don't be too proud to start at the bottom. (You might think about looking for an internship.) Whether it's sports marketing, record-label production, or a television shoot, you're ready and able to do whatever it takes to learn the business. If this involves fulfilling lunch orders and playing messenger, then that's your job for a while. The talent takes up all the available prima donna space in these industries.

- Even the business types need to be flexible and willing to assume responsibility in areas usually outside their domain. Emphasize your organizational skills. In the final analysis, all of these productions—ball games, music events, television shows, movies—require a fanatical attention to detail. If you can remember everything on the to-do list with phones ringing, priorities changing, and a forecast for heavy rain, you're the one they'll all want to hire.

- De-emphasize your need to be in control. Unfortunately, most detail-oriented people are not particularly great at letting chips fall where they may. Quite often in this business they fall helter-skelter, and the show, whatever form it may take, must go on. Making the best of a bad situation is key to your long-term success.

UNDERGRADUATES

To land an entry-level position, you must take the initiative. For those fortunate enough to realize their calling while still in school, internships are a great way to gain experience in the industry. Most companies offer them in almost every division. The work is clerical and the pay—if any—is low, but internships are often considered a trial run for permanent employment. And while some companies require that interns receive college credit, many also grant these positions to recent graduates. Keep in mind that landing an internship at a major entertainment company

> **It's not what you know or even whom you know, but who knows you.**

can be extremely difficult. For example, IMG claims to receive more than 1,000 applications each year for only 70 internship slots. So, be as professional and diligent in your internship search as you would be in your job search.

There is no required academic major for people looking to go into entertainment. "In terms of curriculum," says an insider, "pursue your interests, as opposed to taking specialized courses." Entertainment-business degrees do exist, but such programs are often not taken seriously by people in the business. It's far better for you to get a solid grounding in a marketable major such as marketing, accounting, or communications.

Entry-level jobs are available for people without previous experience, but be prepared to do work that you might have thought beneath you. "People with 4-year degrees start as receptionists," says an insider. "You need that degree of academic maturity." Another insider says, "A degree does not get you anywhere." It's what you do after you get the job, not what you studied at school, that will most influence your career path. In sports, a degree is largely essential, and people do respect a sports-business or even kinesiology degree.

MBAS AND OTHER ADVANCED-DEGREE HOLDERS

If you're considering going back to school so you can start your career in entertainment at a higher level, consider one insider's observations: "A graduate degree helps, but not as much as one would expect. You really learn more in the field than in school." Recent MBA and law school graduates should be aware that such degrees do not guarantee anything in the entertainment industry. Although some companies recruit on campus, most job seekers have to pursue positions on their own. MBAs and law school graduates can expect to start as assistants in the marketing, finance, and legal departments, or in more creative departments such as production and distribution. "You need to work your way up from the bottom," says an insider.

This is less true in sports, where a JD can earn you a slot in an agent-trainee program or as in-house counsel for a league. An MBA is even more prized at the league offices. One insider estimates that a little more than half of the executives in marketing and sales positions in the major leagues have an MBA. "An MBA will only do you good," he says. "You'll advance more quickly and get more interesting projects." A degree in sports management from a good university is extremely useful for team and league positions.

MIDCAREER CANDIDATES

If you have any kind of track record in another industry, prepare to be humbled upon entering the sports and entertainment field. The traditional career path starts at the bottom; your previous experience may not count for much, and may even count against you if you come across as arrogant or unrealistic about your starting opportunities. Your greatest assets will be persistence, good humor, affability, enthusiasm, and the ability to present your talents and experience as a compelling egoless package. And don't forget your crucial network, which you must be creative about building, maintaining, and using.

Before you resign yourself to an "assistant to the coordinator" position, know that some career changers will not have to start at the very bottom. If you have a background in a corporate function like law, finance, accounting, HR, marketing, PR, or sales, you can find similar work in these industries. Again, though, you might have to start at a lower level—manager, rather than director, for example. As always, your best bet is to network, but you have the added advantage when replying to job postings: If Disney or the NFL is looking for accountants, they'll only interview accountants, not any old job seeker. Keep trying hard enough, and eventually you'll land something in your specialty.

Interviewing Tips

Before you start working your contacts and calling up HR departments, get up-to-date on trends in the industry. Consult the trade papers. *The Hollywood Reporter* and *Variety* showcase the entire industry, with an emphasis on television and film, while *Billboard* covers the music industry and *SportsBusiness Journal* covers just what you'd imagine from the title. These publications will educate you on the business as well as give you job leads, whether via classified ads or articles on companies' new or expanding divisions. For sports careers, make sure you keep abreast of your preferred sport and team; you probably are anyway.

Once you have a sense of industry trends, focus on specific jobs. In narrowing your field of target companies, you'll show potential employers that you're serious about the industry. You'll also increase your odds of landing a job—especially if you've done your homework and target jobs in companies or divisions that are performing well in the marketplace.

Every position requires certain skills—take inventory of yours and consider how you can apply them. As an insider says, "More than anything, people need to know that you're capable." And all candidates must be computer savvy. According to an insider, "Microsoft Office is the software du jour. Excel and PowerPoint are also important." Candidates should also know that entertainment companies often use Macintosh systems.

Your next move should be to contact everyone you know (or know of) in the companies or organizations you're interested in. Contact these people to set up informational interviews. Ask them if they know of job openings or other people in the industry you can talk to. At the same time you should call the companies' job hot lines or visit their career websites. Companies accept resumes for positions that have not been posted, but your chances of being contacted are much, much greater if you apply for a particular job. If the hot lines don't yield a suitable listing, contact an HR official for an informational interview. (Be aware, though, that some companies will not schedule such interviews.) One great technique is to apply for a job, and then immediately and very politely ask a contact who also has pull with the hiring manager to put in a good word for you. Be gracious if he or she turns down your request.

A final note: Although only a select group of staffing agencies specializes in the entertainment industry, most major temporary agencies serve entertainment companies. Temps are often hired for permanent positions.

Getting Grilled

Here are examples of the questions you're likely to be asked in your interviews. If you prepare for these, you'll have an easier time with other questions.

- Why do you want to work in the sports or entertainment industry? Why do you want to work for us in particular?

- You have a significant amount of experience. Will you be happy in a job at this level?

- What do you see as the biggest challenge in this position?

- Why should I hire you as opposed to another candidate?

- Discuss specific skills you have that are necessary for this job.

- What are your short- and long-term goals?

- What are good resources for information on the industry?

- Describe the current state of the industry and tell me where you see it headed.

- What kinds of trends make this an exciting industry for you?

Grilling Your Interviewer

The following are good general questions that suit most entertainment company interviews. You'll want to think of questions that apply specifically to the companies with which you're interviewing.

- I've read the job description, but what do you think is the single most important attribute for the job, and why?

- What sort of hours are expected?

- Do you generally promote from within? Can you describe the career path in this department?

- Can employees move laterally between divisions? Can they move laterally between subsidiaries of the parent company?

- What competitive advantages do you have? What areas could use improvement?

- What's your company's overall business strategy? What's your strategy for this division?

- What's the biggest challenge or priority you face?

- How are the company's divisions integrated? (Or, if the company focuses on one or two segments: How are you responding to the trend toward vertical integration in the industry? Do you have industry partnerships?)

- How is your company making use of new media and new ways to deliver entertainment products?

The Final Word

Love the glamour in sports and entertainment, but hate the grunt work? Enjoy the competition, but can't stomach the pay? Comparing sports and entertainment with industries that attract the same types of people, or that provide similar work environments, can help you determine if a job in the entertainment industry is really right for you, or if you'd be happier elsewhere.

Advertising may be entertainment's closest cousin. In fact, many people work in both fields—directors who make commercials and films, actors and athletes who appear on commercials and television shows, musicians who record CDs and provide soundtracks for commercials and movies. Companies in both fields attract creative young turks and pay low wages at the outset, but offer substantial compensation to those who rise to the executive ranks.

Entertainment, however, is far more entrepreneurial than advertising. While ad agency employees often ascend the corporate ladder over a number of years, entertainment employees face something more like a corporate trampoline—one day you're at the bottom, and the next you're at the top. And the turnover rate for film, television, and music executives is much higher than for ad agency executives, who enjoy the additional security of easier transfer to other industries should they decide to bail out of advertising. (To learn more, check out the WetFeet Insider Guide to *Careers in Advertising and Public Relations*.)

Public relations, too, has similarities to entertainment and sports. PR professionals operate in the same general arena—media—and many entertainment and sports companies have PR departments of their own. Beyond that, both fields require communications skills and sensitivity to changing tastes. The skills PR professionals use to draft press releases, propose story ideas, and promote clients and their products in the media are similar to those entertainment executives use—particularly in film and television—to evaluate and summarize prospective scripts, pitch ideas for future projects, and publicize artists and projects. In PR as in entertainment, while entry-level positions pay poorly, executives are well compensated. And PR professionals also struggle to be taken seriously by industry outsiders. But PR offers a clearer path for career advancement, while entertainment is more innovative and dynamic, with a more liberal working environment.

If you're a media junkie or just looking for a fast-paced, innovative field, there are options that might be more appealing to you than entertainment. But when it comes to the glamour factor, there's no topping the entertainment and sports industry. If you have a passion for hobnobbing with "the talent" and pulling the strings behind the next pop-culture sensation or superstar athlete, the low starting pay, job instability, and big egos in entertainment and sports may be a small price to pay.

For Your Reference

Industry Lingo

Recommended Reading

Additional Resources

About the Author

Industry Lingo

Success in entertainment and sports depends in large part on knowing who's who and what's what, so you'd best familiarize yourself with the lexicon. Here's a list of key terms to get you started.

A-list. Hollywood's best and brightest; used in discussing actors, writers, directors, and producers.

Above the line. All expenditures before film or TV production, such as the costs of buying a script and hiring directors and actors. Production costs are "below the line."

Blockbuster. A movie that requires many millions of dollars to make (these days, often upwards of $100 million) but has the potential to return many millions more in box office grosses. Inspired by Steven Spielberg's 1975 hit *Jaws*, which had moviegoers lining up around the block to get into theaters.

Coverage. A brief synopsis and critique of a prospective film script. Typically, interns, production assistants, script readers, or development executives provide coverage.

Dailies. When a film is shooting on location, the dailies—tapes of all the film shot each day—are sent to the movie's producer.

Drop. Taken from hip-hop slang, "to drop" refers to an album's release. It is often used by people in the industry without regard to genre: "The Kansas box set drops at the end of the month? You think you can score me a copy?"

Ears. The ability to spot music talent that others might overlook: "Clive Davis still has great ears."

File sharing. The sharing of computer files, often containing audio or video, among disparate users. The film and music industries are actively lobbying the government to clamp down on peer-to-peer file sharing.

Free agent. A player whose contract has expired and who has the right to negotiate and sign with another team. A restricted free agent is one whose most recent team maintains the right of first refusal, usually with some conditions beneficial to the player attached.

Game book. A yearbook put out by a team for its fans to purchase.

Game day. A day when a team is playing a home game.

Game notes. Player and team stats, biographies, notable recent events—basically anything a team's PR staff thinks will be useful to reporters compiled into one handy package.

Gold. A record "goes gold" when it sells half a million units. It goes platinum when it sells a million units. These awards are issued by the RIAA.

Green light. A studio's go-ahead to make a film. Also used as a verb: "They've green-lighted the sequel to *Armageddon*."

Indie. Film and music industry shorthand for a project made outside the major studio or record-label systems. Most major labels and studios have indie-like subsidiaries for nonmainstream artists and films.

Merchandising. Using a recognizable property—band name, film character, sports logo—to differentiate and sell consumer goods such as clothing, toys, or even automobiles.

mp3. Short for MPEG audio layer-3, the compression technology used to make digital audio files smaller while maintaining high quality. Musicians and fans use mp3 technology to post music files on the Internet for listeners to download.

Naming rights. A form of corporate sponsorship that allows the sponsor to attach its name to a sports facility or event. The comprehensibility spectrum ranges from the relatively straightforward Staples Center (home to several of L.A.'s pro teams) to Major League Soccer's cumbersome got milk? 3v3 Soccer Shootout.

Option. The right to buy a script or story outright within a prescribed time—usually 3 to 5 years. The person whose script or story has been optioned receives a payment up front, plus an additional payment if the project is purchased outright later.

Package. A strategy made famous by former Disney Studios head Michael Ovitz when he was at CAA and considered Hollywood's most powerful agent. When a producer or studio is burning to get a particular script or talent for a project, the agent involved packages that script or talent with other clients (actors, directors, writers). Packaging actors for television can earn agents or agencies 5 to 10 percent of a show's gross for its entire life span.

Pilot. A test episode or episodes of a television show made in the hopes that a network will order the show for an entire season.

Pitch. The process of proposing a script or film idea to producers or studio executives. Satirized hilariously in Robert Altman's *The Player*.

Programming. The process of developing television shows and airing them in the optimum time slots, usually based on the time slots' demographics.

Spec script. A script written on the speculation that someone will buy it.

Special markets. The division of a music label that creates custom CDs for corporate clients, who then distribute them to their customers.

Sweeps. Periods in which Nielsen Media Research compiles data on how television shows rate by demographic category. Networks and channels base their ad rates on the results of sweeps, which happen four times a year.

Tie-in. A sports or entertainment promotion involving another company's product or services. Marketing a sports event on a soda can would be an example.

Treatment. A 4- to 20-page outline of a potential film or television show describing the characters and plot structure in detail. Screenwriters sometimes write treatments rather than an entire spec script.

20/20 club. A select group of actors who can command a $20 million salary up front and 20 percent of the domestic box-office gross on the back end. Jim Carrey, Tom Cruise, Leonardo DiCaprio, Harrison Ford, Mel Gibson, and Tom Hanks are among the 20/20 members.

Recommended Reading

FILM, TELEVISION, AND MUSIC

"Secret Agent Man"

This profile of William Morris Agency president Dave Wirtschafter peers into the inner sanctum of Hollywood deal- and star-making. Perhaps Wirtschafter revealed too much: following its publication, some of his clients were up in arms about his comments, and Sarah Michelle Geller summarily fired him.

Source: Tad Friend, *The New Yorker*, **3/21/05.**

"SBC: One Big Bad Baby Bell"

SBC is betting that Microsoft's Internet protocol television (IPTV) technology will protect it from the cable companies that have been encroaching on its territory by providing phone service. The company, in partnership with Yahoo!, plans to launch a suite of telephone, Internet, and video services that will turn TVs into computers, allowing users customized, on-demand viewing. If successful, this telecom company will end up a major player in the entertainment industry.

Source: Stephanie N. Mehta, *Fortune*, **3/7/05.**

"Not Much to Sing About"

This article provides a good overview of current trends in the music industry.

Source: Ethan Smith, *Wall Street Journal*, 1/31/05.

"Music Business in Misery"

Still want to work for a major label? This depressing roundup of the music industry's woes may make you reconsider.

Source: Jenny Eliscu, RollingStone.com, 8/18/03.

"What Albums Join Together, Everyone Tears Asunder"

Will iTunes save the music industry? This article argues that it could help kill it.

Source: John Pareles, *New York Times*, 7/20/03.

"Who's That Girl?"

Ever wondered how disposable pop stars are manufactured? This lengthy profile of wanna-be superstar Amanda Latona shows her handlers trying to create a persona for her in a way that just might turn your stomach. Though she failed to release an album, similar makeovers have recently been attempted for Liz Phair and Jewel.

Source: Lynn Hirschberg, *New York Times Magazine*, 8/4/02.

"File Sharing: Innocent Until Proven Guilty"

This interview with copyright expert Stan Liebowitz touches on many of the basic points of the file-sharing debate.

Source: Damien Cave, *Salon*, 6/13/02.

"The Future of Television"

This must-read multipart special report touches on some of the programming, technology, and business-strategy trends that will play out over the next decade.

Source: Marc Gunther, *Fortune*, 4/1/02.

"Artists, Insiders Speculate about Effects of Universal/Polygram Merger as D-Day Comes"

Though rather old, this article offers an honest look at what happens to artists and employees as a result of consolidation and cost-cutting.

Source: MTV.com, 1/22/99.

"Broadcast Network Executives Struggle to Reinvigorate Their Business"

If you're looking for a job in the television industry, you need to read this article. It delves into the changing state of a business once dominated by the broadcast networks and now supported by the growth of cable endeavors.

Source: Bill Carter, *New York Times*, 1/4/99.

"The Player's Club"

Depending on your personality, this article will either excite or dampen your desire to work in the film industry. It examines the more corporate structure Hollywood has adopted in recent years, and also covers the industry's enduring traditions, such as networking.

Source: Patrick Goldstein, *Los Angeles Times*, 3/22/98.

"A Day in the Life of a Gofer"

Although the production assistant profiled here has a famous pedigree (he's John Wayne's grandson), he had to start at the bottom like just almost everyone else in Tinsel Town. The article follows him through a day's work.

Source: Gali Kronenberg, *Los Angeles Times*, 3/24/97.

SPORTS

"Sailing Away with Sports Marketing"

This interview with Doug Augustine, COO of Octagon, provides a good look at the personality traits that make a successful sports marketer.

Source: *SportsBusiness International*, 8/04.

"Agent Is Tackling a Huge Workload"

This rundown of IMG agent Tom Condon's numerous deals and negotiations provides a look at the staggering amount and variety of work a successful sports agent deals with.

Source: Michael Smith, *The Boston Globe*, 2/22/04.

"MJ Remains a Sought-After Endorsement Prize"

This article highlights the full arc of pitchman-extraordinaire Michael Jordan's endorsement career.

Source: Darren Rovell, ESPN.com, 12/31/03.

"Corporations Seek X-Factor"

A generation of do-it-yourselfers with little interest in pro sports has emerged. This article shows how corporations can reach these action-sports aficionados.

Source: Conor Dougherty, SignOnSanDiego.com, 7/27/03.

"The Biggest Crapshoot in Sports"

Will 19-year-old LeBron James be the endorsement king that Michael Jordan was? Nike, Adidas, and a lot of other companies think so.

Source: Ronald Grover, with Stanley Holmes, BusinessWeek.com, 5/5/03.

"Sports Score Big Online"

TV is still the dominant media for sports, but Web-based broadcasts could give sports organizations as much as 15 percent of their revenue by 2004.

Source: Alex Salkever, BusinessWeek.com, 4/15/03.

"The NFL Machine"

This is a good overview of the NFL, focusing on Commissioner Paul Tagliabue's efforts to make the NFL not just a sports business, but also an integrated entertainment business.

Source: Tom Lowry, BusinessWeek.com, 1/27/03.

"Inside the Stadium Name-Rights Business"

This is an overview of the thinking that should go behind entering into a stadium name-rights agreement; includes a .pdf report card that grades the effectiveness of more than 50 pro sports-related naming-rights deals.

Source: Dan Lippe, AdAge.com, 10/28/02.

"It's All About the Benjamins"

This first-person account, written by a lawyer turned sports agent, is a must-read for anyone considering this field.

Source: Allan Wade, MemphisBar.org, 3/02.

"Free-Agent Frenzy: A Day in the Life of an NFL Agent"

Though endorsements are the real pot of gold in pro sports, players need to play to earn them. And to play, they need good contracts with teams. This article shows what an agent's day is like during the busiest time of the year.

Source: Len Pasquarelli, CBSSportsline.com, 2/12/00.

Additional Resources

BOOKS

Down and Dirty Pictures:
Miramax, Sundance, and the Rise of Independent Film

Peter Biskind (Simon & Schuster, 2004)

This tell-all bestseller covers the exhilarating period in the late '80s and early '90s during which independent filmmakers had a major impact on the mass market. The juicy gossip will keep you flipping the pages, but the stomach-turning tales of short-sightedness, greed, and betrayal may make you reconsider movies as a desirable career option.

Adventures in the Screen Trade

William Goldman (Warner Books, 1994)

Although it was written by a screenwriter for screenwriters, this book is valuable for its explanation of the entire process of filmmaking, from drafting a script to production. It's also the source of the most famous quote regarding the movie business: "Nobody knows anything."

All You Need to Know About the Music Business

Donald S. Passman (Simon & Schuster, 2003)

Though aimed at musicians, this classic guide will give anyone interested in the industry a superbly detailed overview to the inner workings of record deals, publishing, and even motion picture music.

Exploding: The Highs, Hits, Hype, Heroes, and Hustlers of the Warner Music Group

Stan Cornyn (Harper Entertainment, 2002)

This irreverent tell-all account of the rise of Warner Music Group—written by a former Warner executive—will give you a good idea of the surprisingly fast-and-free approach major labels took (or used to take) to marketing and selling music.

Hit & Run

Nancy Griffin and Kim Masters (Touchstone, 1996)

This book chronicles what industry insiders describe as "the most public screwing in the history of the business." The authors describe how Jon Peters and Peter Guber became studio executives, produced some of the most successful films of the past 2 decades, and subsequently took Sony Corporation for hundreds of millions of dollars.

Hit Men: Power Brokers & Fast Money Inside the Music Business

Fredric Dannen (Times Books, 1990)

This exceedingly sordid and entertaining tale of the music industry focuses on "promotion men," a small group of grifters who inserted themselves in between the record companies and the radio stations. Excellent background reading.

The Ultimate Guide to Sports Marketing

Stedman Graham et al. (McGraw Hill Trade, 2001)

This overview of sports marketing includes sections on event promotions, licensing deals, and how to attract and keep sponsors.

Sports Law: A Desktop Handbook

Paul M. Anderson (National Sports Law Institute, 1999)

This reference book covers 11 areas of sports law, including merchandising and licensing, facilities, torts, and labor law.

Winning With Integrity:
Getting What You Want Without Selling Your Soul

Leigh Steinberg, Michael D'Orso (Times Books, 1999)
This is a step-by-step look at all stages of negotiation by one of the top sports agents.

The Dream Job: Sports Publicity, Promotion and Marketing (3rd ed)

Melvin Heliter (University Sports Press, 1999)
This book on sports careers has become a staple of sport-business classes across the country.

DIRECTORIES

Hollywood Creative Directory

Updated every several months, the *Hollywood Creative Directory* lists personnel at film studios, production companies, and television channels and networks.

U.S. Directory of Entertainment Employers

This reference provides contact information for major entertainment companies. It has listings for companies in related industries, from ad agencies to video distributors. It also includes recruiters, film commissions, trade associations, and publications. Entertainment Employment Journal Publishers Group publishes a newsletter that profiles jobs in the industry. Check the company's website (www.eej.com) for details on these and other references.

TRADE JOURNALS

Industry executives live and die by what's printed in these trade publications. Although subscription rates are high, the information in them is more in-depth than what you'll find in traditional business resources. The following are some of the key ones to read:

Billboard (www.billboard.com)

Daily Variety and *Variety* (www.variety.com)

The Hollywood Reporter (www.hollywoodreporter.com)

SportsBusiness Journal (www.sportsbusinessjournal.com)

TRADE ASSOCIATIONS

These associations provide general information on the state of the film, television, and music industries:

Motion Picture Association of America (www.mpaa.org)

Recording Industry Association of America (www.riaa.com)

JOB BOARDS AND RESOURCE WEBSITES

4entertainmentjobs.com (www.4entertainmentjobs.com)

EntertainmentCareers.Net (www.entertainmentcareers.net)

EntertainmentJobs.com (www.eej.com)

FilmBiz (www.filmbiz.com)

National Association of Recording Industry Professionals (www.narip.com)

National Sports Forum (www.sports-forum.com)

Showbizjobs (www.showbizjobs.com)

Sports Careers (www.sportscareers.com)

The Velvet Rope (www.velvetrope.com)

Work in Sports (www.workinsports.com)

RESOURCES FOR WOMEN AND MINORITIES

The following organizations provide insight into various segments of the industry for women and minorities, and in some cases mentoring for aspiring industry workers. Some also have job listings.

American Women in Radio & Television (www.awrt.org)

Association for Women in Communications Inc. (www.womcom.org)

Black Filmmaker Foundation (www.dvrepublic.com)

National Association of Minorities in Cable (www.namic.com)

New York Women in Film & Television (www.nywift.org)

Women in Cable & Telecommunications Inc. (www.wict.org)

Women in Film (www.wif.org)

Women in Sports Careers Foundation (www.wiscfoundation.org)

Women Sports Jobs (www.womensportsjobs.com)

EMPLOYMENT AGENCIES

The following employment agencies were endorsed by a human resources manager at a Los Angeles–based entertainment conglomerate. Similar agencies exist in New York.

All-Star Agency
9663 Santa Monica Boulevard
Beverly Hills, CA 90210
Phone: 310-271-5217

AppleOne
325 West Broadway
Glendale, CA 91204
Phone: 818-247-2991

Friedman Personnel Agency
9000 W. Sunset Boulevard, Suite 1000
West Hollywood, CA 90069
Phone: 310-550-1002

About the Author

J. Michael Ribas lives in Pasadena, California. In 2002, he left WetFeet, where he held several positions in the Content and Web departments, and moved to Los Angeles, to break into the music industry. He currently handles music marketing for a broad-based entertainment company.

WETFEET'S INSIDER GUIDE SERIES

Job Search Guides

Getting Your Ideal Internship

Job Hunting A to Z: Landing the Job You Want

Killer Consulting Resumes!

Killer Cover Letters & Resumes!

Killer Investment Banking Resumes!

Negotiating Your Salary & Perks

Networking Works!

Interview Guides

Ace Your Case: Consulting Interviews

Ace Your Case II: 15 More Consulting Cases

Ace Your Case III: Practice Makes Perfect

Ace Your Case IV: The Latest & Greatest

Ace Your Case V: Return to the Case Interview

Ace Your Interview!

Beat the Street: Investment Banking Interviews

Beat the Street II: I-Banking Interview Practice Guide

Career & Industry Guides

Careers in Accounting

Careers in Advertising & Public Relations

Careers in Asset Management & Retail Brokerage

Careers in Biotech & Pharmaceuticals

Careers in Brand Management

Careers in Consumer Products

Careers in Entertainment & Sports

Careers in Health Care

Careers in Human Resources

Careers in Information Technology

Careers in Investment Banking

Careers in Management Consulting

Careers in Marketing & Market Research

Careers in Nonprofits & Government Agencies

Careers in Real Estate

Careers in Retail

Careers in Supply Chain Management

Careers in Venture Capital

Industries & Careers for MBAs

Industries & Careers for Undergrads

Specialized Consulting Careers: Health Care, Human Resources, and Information Technology

Company Guides

25 Top Consulting Firms

25 Top Financial Services Firms

Accenture

Bain & Company

Booz Allen Hamilton

Boston Consulting Group

Credit Suisse First Boston

Deloitte Consulting

The Goldman Sachs Group

J.P. Morgan Chase & Co.

Lehman Brothers

McKinsey & Company

Merrill Lynch & Co.

Morgan Stanley

UBS

WetFeet in the City Guides

Job Hunting in New York City

Job Hunting in San Francisco